I MET HIM
IN MY
OVERALLS

I MET HIM
IN MY
OVERALLS

Life Lessons from the Master Gardener

JEAN COLEMAN

Pleasant Word (a division of WinePress Publishing, PO Box 428, Enumclaw, WA 98022) functions only as book publisher. As such, the ultimate design, content, editorial accuracy, and views expressed or implied in this work are those of the author.

Unless otherwise noted, all Scriptures are taken from *The New American Standard Bible*, © 1960, 1963, 1968, 1971, 1972, 1973, 1975, 1977 by The Lockman Foundation. Used by permission.

Scripture references marked NIV are taken from the *Holy Bible, New International Version®, NIV®*. Copyright © 1973, 1978, 1984 by Biblica, Inc.™ Used by permission of Zondervan. All rights reserved worldwide.

Scripture references marked MSG are taken from *The Message Bible* © 1993 by Eugene N. Peterson, NavPress, PO Box 35001, Colorado Springs, CO 80935, 4th printing in USA 1994. Published in association with the literary agency—Alive Comm. PO Box 49068, Colorado Springs, CO 80949. Used by permission.

Scripture references marked KJV are taken from the *King James Version* of the Bible.

Scripture references marked NLT are taken from the *Holy Bible, New Living Translation*, copyright © 1996, 2004 by Tyndale Charitable Trust. Used by permission of Tyndale House Publishers, Wheaton, Illinois 60189. All rights reserved.

Music:
Song Title: GIVE THEM ALL TO JESUS
Writer credits: Phil Johnson and Bob Benson
Copyright: 1975 Dimension Music (admin. By BMG Music) SESAC

Names and details in some of the stories have been changed to protect the identities of the persons involved.

ISBN 13: 978-1-4141-1385-2
ISBN 10: 1-4141-1385-4
Library of Congress Catalog Card Number: 2009901095

To my children (including those who are now mine through vows),
And their children (those present and those not yet arrived),
And their children's children:

I would give you the keys to my kingdom if I had one, but instead
I give you the key to my heart. All that God has given me is stored
there for you.

Her children rise up and bless her.
—Prov. 31:28

CONTENTS

ACKNOWLEDGMENTS

Wigth HUMBLE APPRECIATION, I thank my husband, who is most singularly responsible for my search for personal authenticity and for my present relationship with Jesus. He drove me to my knees, questioned my motives, and forced me to examine, re-examine, and examine again my faith and choices! He is a man of unique talent, energy, humor, and spirit. I have great regard for his insight. I have loved him since I was sixteen years old when we walked high school corridors together. He has been both my best friend and my toughest critic along life's path, and I am unquestionably stronger for having shared the journey with my handsome husband. Lastly, he afforded me the opportunity, privilege, and blessing of living here at Cowlick Farm. I am profoundly grateful.

My dad, by being kind, generous, and loving, made it easy for me to accept a heavenly Father who loves me unconditionally. To have known his love and to have witnessed his adoration of my mother places me among the very blessed of this earth. He graced those around him with his humor, personality, and warm spirit, and he left a permanent imprint on my heart.

When I was young, my mom encouraged my sisters and me to learn and recite Bible verses. It was a challenge to be sure, and I perhaps did it to win her favor rather than God's. But many of those verses took root and continue to grow deep within my spirit. They are like an automatic watering system that comes on when needed. They have great sustaining power. Thank you, Mom, for planting those seeds in me.

It has been a blessing to share the memories of childhood with my two sisters, each viewing our journey from differing perspectives. They patiently reminisced with me as I probed their insights while exploring my own depths. I relish the laughs we share along the way and I thank God for them.

More than in any other way, God used my three children to teach me about my relationship to Him. It is a privilege to be their mom, and I am immeasurably richer for it. Thank you, Katie, Jim Barr, and Taylor, for decorating my life with your innate beauty.

When I began the initial process of market gardening, it was my friend Carol who partnered with me. Had she not shared my desire to hoe, row, sow, grow, and know, I wouldn't have attempted the process! We combined our limited knowledge, available tools, and a commitment of time to begin the undertaking. We shared much laughter, a few tears, and many pulled muscles, aches, and pains as well as daily discouragement and excitement. Gardening with her doubled the fun and halved the work. Thank you, Carol.

My fondest thanks to Melissa, who printed and reprinted the many editions of my manuscript as I fumbled through the process of writing. She so patiently helped me with the technological process where I was quite deficient. I expect to see little white wings sprout on her before long.

Betsy, my dear friend who gave her time unselfishly in the early editing of my fledgling manuscript, was a blessing covered in flesh. Her offer to help was an answer to prayer. Forever and ever, I will love and praise God for the gift of her.

On the eve of releasing the final manuscript for publication, I was battling doubts and discouragement, suffering from (what I hear is every) author's angst. While sitting at my computer, my friend Katherine called and, as if on cue, encouraged me to press on. Sensing my labor pains from afar, she exhorted me to persevere and birth this book. Her love and friendship have sustained me. She has been a portrait of grace. Thank you, Katherine.

FOREWORD

I SPECIFICALLY REMEMBER saying to my mother as an eager teenager, "But I don't want any wisdom. I don't want to be wise. I just want to have fun right now." As ridiculous as this sounds, it's true. And more humiliating, I specifically remember saying this more than once—no, more than ten times. Could it be even a hundred times? Oh dear, I dread the thought. Nevertheless, the wisdom flowed. From girlfriends to boyfriends, career plans to childbirths, disappointments to triumphs, my mom and the author of this book dispensed pearl upon pearl of wisdom. And though I may not have heeded her direction, and most often did not, these pearls were taken into my heart by God's grace and now speak to me daily.

By simply being in the presence of another, so much is learned. God is so good in that He promises blessing upon blessing if we would just abide in Him. I believe that in striving to be the perfect mother, wife, teacher, gardener, and friend (among other endeavors), my mom so clung to God's guidance that I somehow received the blessing as well. Though her struggles were real and her own heartaches poignant, her deep faith was ever present.

And from that faith, peace, joy, and wisdom *always* overflowed from Mom.

The lessons I learned from her have become the very foundation of my faith. They are the truths I cling to as I raise my own children, as I try to be a godly wife to my own husband, and as I seek God in my own life. These pearls of wisdom have been my greatest blessing. They are my greatest inheritance.

And so, when my mother asked me to write the foreword to her book, it was an easy decision. How fitting that I—the recipient of all these life lessons—offer an introduction to the very truths that now make me who I am. Reader, let me say this about what lies beyond this page: there is the story of a woman who worked so hard to be so many things to so many people, a woman much like you or me or your own sister or mother. There is the revelation of a God who longs to meet us wherever we are, a God who longs to dig in the dirt, fold laundry, or drive a carpool right along side us. And there are life lessons—pearl upon pearl—given from God to my mom, a dear Southern woman who one day decided to put on her overalls and grow a garden.

I pray for every reader now that your heart would be open to receive some pearls of your own. Our God is faithful, and His words are true. Let His wisdom find you, and you will be blessed.

—Katie Koon

INTRODUCTION

I T WAS THREE A.M. The unmistakable scent of a baby filled the dimly lit room. Every square inch of my body ached with fatigue. My heavy eyelids begged to stay shut as my sore back pleaded for rest. Barely conscious, I stuck one arm out of bed to rock the bassinet that held my newborn grandson.

He was my daughter's first, and I was there to help in any way possible. After his third day of new world adjustment, he squirmed and fussed for most of the night. The bassinet's slight movement temporarily eased his distress. At this pre-dawn hour, I wanted to extend his momma's limited moments of sleep before feeding time. Sitting up, I continued to rock his little bed rhythmically as I prayed for him.

In an attempt to revive myself, I praised God for the miracle of birth. Putting my words of thanksgiving to music, I composed a lullaby using a familiar tune. While softly singing, a Holy Presence seemed to surround me. I was both humbled and overwhelmed with the blessing of sharing this pivotal time with my daughter as she joined my world of motherhood.

Baby Henry's discomfort increased. I tried rocking, walking, and holding him in every imaginable position. I knew of nothing else in the physical realm to do for my little fretful companion. I would have given my very life for this tiny new creation, or his mother, if necessary. Kneeling, I submitted my grandson to God, asking, "Lord, what can I do? What can I give him?" Almost immediately, I felt summoned, as if by an unseen roommate or an imperceptible hearing in my spirit: "Give him Me."

The Divine Voice does not always express itself with words. Sometimes it is a heart-consciousness. In that unexpected moment, I felt a strong, inner exhortation to transcribe all I believed God had revealed to me. My heart was full and overflowing. With mixed feelings of reverence, timidity, and wonder, I glanced around the room, looking for confirmation. Had someone entered unawares?

Though it was not an audible voice, I knew at once that it was the answer to my plea and that, as a grandmother, it was time to tell my story. It is not unusual, riveting, or impressive in any particular way, but it is mine. Everyone has a story and there is something to be learned from each.

Having seen God in a personal way while growing flowers for market, I was accustomed to witnessing Him in the ordinary occurrences of life. Many mysteries had unfolded in simple, everyday circumstances, like lighting a match and seeing objects in a pitch-black room. Each revelation, like each object lit up in the darkness, is a gift from God, and I want to share from the abundance I received. Though I am not a writer, I vowed to my Caller, in the wee hours of that sleepless morning, to do just that. Gazing at my grandbaby through misty eyes, I fervently committed to record the revelations.

Life managed to get in the way, and I postponed the undertaking for nearly two years. A potentially fatal accident (shared in Chapter 22) brought the purpose of my life into clear focus, and I recommitted myself to answer "the call." Being out of commission taught me to hold more loosely those things I commanded before.

I have not been the same since that accident. I think more about eternity now. How interesting it is that in the flesh, as old age approaches, our bodies tend to broaden in width and decrease in height. I am witnessing that in my physical body for sure. However, in the spiritual realm, what has been a very horizontal life is becoming more vertical daily. I spent a lifetime looking to the right and left for answers. I now look up to God and, ultimately, to Him alone.

I am acutely aware of my inability to express adequately what is supernatural. God's awesome enormity cannot be defined by mortal words. Attempting to interpret what He has impressed on my heart has been overwhelming, but the insights I received are as crown jewels I want to bequeath. I realize I actually possess nothing else of lasting value to give. With a thankful heart, I pass along these blessings to my children, grandchildren, and any with ears to hear. For if the angst I felt in life can be used for good, then nothing has been suffered in vain.

P.S. Since that midnight summons and the subsequent beginning of this writing, three more bundles from heaven have arrived, and more are on the way. Therefore, I have at least four additional reasons to press on.

Chapter 1

HIDE AND SEEK

Seek, and you will find.

—Matt. 7:7

Preschool: Feeling Shame

IT WAS A September afternoon, and my imaginary friends, Estelle and Son-a-dun-dun, hunched under my parents' bed with me. My heart raced with fear of being discovered. I'd stolen my sister's allowance—a quarter—and I knew if I got caught I'd be punished, which was my greatest fear. I hated being chastised. Mom eventually found me and issued a verbal reproof. I sought solace among my dolls in the familiarity of my room.

My invisible playmates, as close and real to me as my skin, played a strategic part in my existence. Later that year, on a cold winter morning, we discovered a heat vent under the bed, and we held a thermometer over the warm duct in hopes of raising the mercury to a feverish mark. Remembering that a high fever produced concern from both parents, I claimed sickness, but I needed tangible proof. My motive was to spend the morning at home alone with my mom—to get the undivided attention I longed for but rarely received being the youngest of three daughters. Instead, I earned another reprimand—this time from Dad—for attempting to deceive her. Thankfully, Estelle and Son-a-dun-dun shared each rebuke with me and knew the depth of my loneliness and the ache in my spirit.

Little memory of that early, pre-kindergarten period remains other than the vague sense of shame I felt for being the unacceptable person I believed I was.

Grade School: Falling Short

Bonnie, my best grade-school friend, was a pretty blonde and an important character (with visible skin) in the story of my young life. We shared a nearly perfect friendship. Alternating houses, we spent most afternoons playing "grown-up" with a passion. We took our pretend roles as mommies very seriously. During family vacations, I let Bonnie baby-sit my doll, Martha Sue. I gave detailed instructions regarding her care, including the make-believe foods she should eat at each meal while I was away. Along with a suitcase of doll clothes and baby accessories, I parked a pink metal high chair strategically in her family's breakfast room.

When we went shopping with Mom, she lovingly introduced Bonnie, saying, "Isn't she pretty?" Mom singled out Bonnie to the gas station attendant and complimented her to the grocer. She even exalted her beauty when we visited my grandmother. The shop owners recognized me, so I needed no introduction with them. Though I knew this, Mom's praise of Bonnie still stung, and the dishonor of feeling second best lingered like the aftertaste of sour milk. I had short, straight black hair with blunt-cut bangs. I felt un-pretty and disregarded. Unimportant. It was surely no conscious fault of my mom's, yet I considered myself inferior to my best friend. I never doubted my mother's love, but I longed for her praise. Nothing seemed to clear my hazy self-image permanently.

Junior High: Lock It Up

This haziness resurfaced years later, when, in junior high school, I stood in the principal's office, waiting for his response to my lie. I stealthily had carved my initials in the table at the library, using a book I pretended to read as a protective screen. The librarian later discovered the fresh engraving, remembered me sitting at that table, and reported me. I harbored an indescribable humiliation as I stood in the revered office, knees weak and almost blind with horror. (Nice girls weren't sent to the principal's office.) I barely could get the words of denial out of my mouth. My tongue betrayed me, abruptly abandoning its ability to function. My head throbbed and seemed to swell with each heartbeat as embarrassment forced blood to my face. The secretary, office assistant, and other potential informants surely saw it turn ugly shades of red and likely felt waves emitting from my mortification. I must have radiated heat, like black asphalt in the summer sun. Nevertheless, I denied any guilt and, therefore, was not punished, though the damage to my self-respect was greater than any disciplinary action the principal could have administered.

In that degrading moment, I subconsciously entered into an agreement with myself. I couldn't go back to all those people and tell the truth about my lie. Never would I divulge the shady person that cowered behind my smile. I wanted to keep her out of sight in order to maintain my good reputation. She, who nobody knew, was now a liar as well as a juvenile thief. I created a personal dungeon to hide my unacceptable behavior and the sickening uneasiness it created in me. The daunting realization of my capacity for sin, made blatant to me by the outright lie, was frightening, so I stuffed it in the dark cell and locked it up, out of sight.

High School: Out of Sight, Out of Mind

Since I'd effectively pushed the debilitating disappointment in myself out of mind, a couple of years later when I inadvertently shoplifted a swimsuit from a local department store, I easily justified my actions.

Having taken several suits home for parental approval, I returned the ones Mom didn't allow. I set the bag of multi-colored swimwear on the counter, and told the clerk which one I wanted to keep. Checking the receipt, she charged the one suit to my parents' account and then credited back all the others. The trusting saleswoman never looked in the bag where one of the swimsuits remained. Realizing her failure to notice, I walked out quietly with a free swimsuit—my second favorite.

I was struck by how easy it was. To this day, I can remember that infamous yellow, white, and black daisy-print two-piece suit. A scary gratification about the crime I had committed came over me, a kind of pleasure/pain response, like scratching a raw, itching wound. Since it was not premeditated, I rationalized the act by blaming the clerk for her oversight rather than taking responsibility for my dishonesty. Having walked the straight and narrow by most standards for nearly all of my life, I reasoned the misdemeanor was OK, even normal.

Aside from my petty theft as a preschooler and lying in junior high, my record was exemplary (as far as anyone could see). Misconduct had not been much of a temptation before. However, as an older teenager, I was oddly proud to have broken the law with my swimsuit heist. I felt adventurous, like a secret rebel. After all, no real harm was done. Many other high schoolers did much worse. Some part of me wanted to experience the forbidden side—the same part that carved the initials. Maybe walking the moral/ethical tightrope had grown tiring and I felt a detour would bring more fun or independence, even relief. I don't really know. Regrettably, I foolishly sabotaged my already fragile self-respect and kept my vow of nondisclosure.

While driving away, a formless, unidentifiable nag in my spirit weighed down my conscience. Suppressing it, I hurried to cheerleading practice.

Except for occasional white lies, typical teenage tomfoolery, and routine everybody-does-it deceptions, my sins were practically unnoticeable to an outsider. I listened to tales of adolescence from my respectable parents and convinced myself that my naughtiness was no worse than theirs. Eager for vindication, I maintained open ears for confessions from others.

The Pendulum Swings

Despite this inward struggle to justify my sin, my heart for the underprivileged in the community developed. Their troubles weighed heavily on me, and I felt ashamed for not helping to ease their plight. Racial injustices were prevalent in the south, and though I was ingrained in the lifestyle, my conscience wrestled with the prejudices surrounding me. Also, knowledge of elementary school bullies picking on poor, helpless underdogs or peers humiliated in my own high school corridors rocked my sense of justice. I longed to even every unfairness. Tethered to an unseen pole of unworthiness, any kind of suffering sparked guilt in me because I lived a protected and privileged life.

My existence seemed like a pendulum, swinging between two extremes. Happiness, success, and confidence haled on one end, while a gnawing incompleteness waited on the other. Never encouraged to probe, much less express, my inner thoughts, I concealed my disappointments, doubts, and fears. I wanted to divulge my secrets to someone else who appeared successful but was guarding personal inmates of his or her own.

Shadow of a Doubt

One Sunday evening during my high school years, I was in my upstairs bedroom mourning the recent unexpected death of a long-time friend. Staring at mortality up close stunned me. Lying across the end of my bed, I remembered my friend and sobbed.

Conversation and laughter emanated from friends and family who had gathered downstairs. Then the distant conversation lapsed momentarily, and Mom called my name. It was time for me to leave for Methodist Youth Fellowship (MYF) but I didn't move, wanting to see what would happen. I could hear family members looking throughout the house and casually reporting, "I don't see her." One searcher even glanced in my room, but from the doorway she didn't see me stretched across the bed. Without stepping inside, she proclaimed, "She's not in here." In the fading daylight, I must have looked like a folded comforter. A couple of minutes later, the hunt ceased, and I heard a voice from the group say, "Oh well … what were we saying?" With the interruption of the brief search over, their chatting resumed quickly. I felt irrelevant, like they had given up on their efforts too easily. I wondered if I would have been missed if I'd been the one who had died. In my weepy state, I decided I soon would have been forgotten.

That incident often resurfaces in my memory. As silly as it may seem, I desperately wanted to be found. That one small occurrence represented the longing of my heart. Not only did I want to be missed, I ached to be diligently searched for, passionately desired, and cherished like a family heirloom. Resembling a young child hiding behind her own little hands in a game of peek-a-boo, I yearned to be discovered. And like the small child, I needed to be reassured I was good—even important.

Empowering the Doubts

On other occasions, I remember jealously watching my daddy spend many hours tutoring my sister in algebra. At the end of the semester when she proudly brought home a passing grade, they celebrated; she danced and he cheered. They spent the evening discussing the exam and how their hours together had paid off.

Later, when I presented my honor roll report card for parental signature, I received a momentary warm smile and a characteristic wink as my dad said, "Pretty work." He dutifully signed the card, handed it back to me, and quietly returned to his newspaper. I said nothing and stuffed my disappointment for the lack of equal praise in the dungeon with shame. (*But she barely passed and I made honor roll—without help. This isn't fair!*)

Another random chink in my self-esteem occurred when, with bridled pride, I announced at the dinner table that I had made head cheerleader for the coming year. "Congratulations! Pass the butter please," was the dismissive response. No merriment or discussion, no hugs or cheers. My achievement held little significance or perhaps was even expected. Feeling disregarded, I avoided eye contact for the rest of the meal. The personal joy of my announcement melted like the butter on my hot biscuit.

It was not until I was an older, wiser adult that I realized I never had expressed my need to my parents. The problem was mine, not theirs. Since I buried my hurts, no one realized how desperately I craved my family's affirmation. Rather than voicing my disappointments honestly, I maintained an excellent performance record, hoping this spontaneously would produce the display of love I so desired.

Instinctively I knew I should enjoy my successes and that the praise of others should not motivate me. I wanted not to care, to ignore these instincts, but I couldn't. Therefore, even my sadness produced guilt. My parents were good, very good, but my thirst was greater.

Years later I read what God said in Jeremiah 31:14, "My people will be satisfied with My goodness." Now I believe what felt like guilt was actually a God-consciousness—the still, small voice of God. I've learned my uneasiness of heart can be instructive, nudging me to detour from my current unhealthy path. As a young person, God was calling me to a righteous satisfaction and a joyful

Christ-centeredness. However, my me-centeredness, caused by unresolved yearnings, bloomed instead, and His call fell on deaf ears. I had no clue about my purpose in life.

Regrettably, I chose to wear the burdensome garb of a victim many times, which shadowed so much joy, rather than sporting the sheer joyousness of a victor. With that mindset, I too frequently viewed my life as cloudy with periods of sunshine, rather than sunny with a few clouds.

Prodigal Daughter?

One thing that helped flesh out my thought process was the parable of the prodigal son (Luke 15:11-32). Initially, I identified with the loyal, good son who had remained at home with the father, dutifully doing his work. From the parable, we assume he did not complain or express any need. He lived a comfortable life, like me. Yet he was angry and jealous when his rebellious brother returned home and received a royal welcome from his father.

As I first read it, I felt the selfish hurt of the devoted son. Perhaps others would identify with the prodigal, rejoicing in the father's grace and forgiveness as well as the returning son's confessed waywardness. But I wanted the son who had stayed home to receive the praise.

The parable is a beautiful portrayal of an earthly father reflecting the heart of our heavenly Father to forgive quickly all who go astray. Illustrating that God's love is beyond justice and reason, it gives us a glimpse of His sacred face. But I focused on the unfairness (again), not realizing I, too, had strayed and squandered the abundant inheritance my heavenly Father had provided me.

With deep sorrow, I began to see myself in both sons, but in a different way. My self-righteousness and lack of joy likened me to the dutiful son, but by not being content with my heavenly Father's sufficiency, I was as the mutinous one. Though not as blatant, my sins were as unrighteous as those of the runaway.

Unlike me, the prodigal set aside his pride to admit failure and return. I had been so preoccupied with climbing the ladder of goodness that I failed to see the truth about me. The more I tried to hide my resentment and disappointment, the harder it was to confess I was hiding at all. Though spurned by good intentions, my elder son behavior actually distanced me from God. Much later, confession led me to repentance, which landed me in God's arms under the shelter of His grace.

My forgiving Father waited for me to come back to Him even before I knew I had left. Grace, by its very nature, isn't fair. It is God's unmerited favor. Not only did I muddy the delight of my youthful accomplishments, I also postponed the lavish welcome home party with my misguided focus.

Trickle-down Christianity

I knew about an almighty God through Sunday school, church, and Christian parents. God-seeds were randomly scattered in my young heart. As a child, an unexplainable, supernatural closeness to who I assumed was God, grew in me. I often walked in the woods behind our house, talking to Someone who, I was sure, heard me.

As a young adult, I accepted that Jesus died for me and that God wanted to have a relationship with me. I trusted He was more than just a big, old, ethereal, cosmic God out there in the great unknown. I made a mental decision and a verbal commitment (more out of a perceived ought-to than want-to) to believe in Him and to trust the Bible as His divine Word. It was like going to college after high school; I never considered any other alternative. A commitment of faith was what a nice person like me, in a religious environment like mine, did.

With my new pledge came the promise that I was a "new creature in Christ Jesus." I was told the old me had died and the new me was "alive through Christ." However, the promised new life failed to create the new me I desperately craved. The slate didn't seem wiped clean at all. My deceiver's marks showed through, like yesterday's lesson poorly erased by the student on blackboard duty. Where was the regeneration and conversion to a fresh being? I had expected an almost magical makeover, like dipping a strawberry into chocolate.

Many reservations about the authenticity of my new assurance emerged. Eerily, they began to resemble my old doubts. Though my spiritual eyes cracked open and the seeds were watered lightly, no new me sprung to life. *Maybe my unworthiness caused the "new creature" that was supposed to have been conceived, to be aborted.*

When my new Christianity hoopla subsided and old patterns returned, the sweater of my life unraveled and wore thin. In time, the repugnance I harbored toward the captives hidden in the neglected dungeon of my soul emerged. I despised their degrading existence, even as I campaigned for the approval of others. I gained popularity with my peers, but liked myself less and less.

Moreover, the loathing spread, like smoke seeping out of a closed room, when I added "hypocrite" to my list of labels. I was a new, enlightened Christian by title, but a deceitful sinner by nature. That leaking smoke clouded my reasoning, the haze blocking my view. I believed not even a loving God could forgive the likes of me. I rationalized I would have to earn my salvation if I wanted to get to heaven. I muscled my way toward perfection, which I hoped would afford relief in the present and passage through the pearly gates eventually. I still didn't know about grace.

I gladly identified with the apostle Paul when I first read his confession, "For I know that nothing good dwells in me, that is, in my flesh; for the willing is present in me, but the doing of the good is not. For the good that I want, I do not do, but I practice the very evil that I do not want" (Rom. 7:18-19). What a comfort to know the notorious Paul of the New Testament and I shared the same dilemma! I wrongly used his confession to reconcile my locked-up self to my good self and to console my dented spirit. Paul gave validity, substance, and influence to my ongoing clandestine struggle. I was in good company, I (pridefully) reassured myself. Maybe I was off the hook and not so bad after all.

Over the years, my Christianity trickled from my head to my soul, where I continued my march for moral correctness. I knew about Jesus, and He was important to me, but something remained unsettled. Having no practical relationship with Jesus or understanding of God's grace created a spiritual deficit in me. The Bible was essentially lifeless, and I secretly struggled with doubts, which fractured the "firm foundation" of my faith. Religion, ironically, was not conducive to the seeds' growth but only to the growth of guilt and judgment. Many Christians seemed artificial and phony. Deep in my privacy, I feared I might be, too.

It took years before I submitted my will, opened my heart to God, and allowed Jesus to come all the way into my inner spaces. I had left Him on the border, not allowing Him full access to my soul.

Chapter 2

HERE COMES THE BRIDE

And the two shall become one flesh.

—Eph. 5:31

FROM ALGEBRA TO Friday night football, to Teenage Club dances, my high school years were full and fun. Charmed. I wore saddle oxfords, circle pins, and bouffant hairdos with pride. Whether doing the cha-cha to Roy Orbison or bopping to the Temptations, I embraced the rhythm of those years. Occasionally my sister and I danced with our pillows while crooning with Elvis in our bedroom at night. Like doing the Hokey Pokey, I plunged my whole self into the drama of high school and twirled in the magic of the mosaic.

Appointed yearbook editor at the end of my junior year, I relished the confidence the staff had in me, but privately thought they could have made a better choice. Even induction into the National Honor Society caused a soulish squirm. The academic grades I earned were mine, but I had cheated on occasion and not confessed. Though I received the honor readily, I felt dishonorable for the secrets I harbored.

In the fall of my senior year, I was honored as homecoming queen. However, perched atop the senior float as it paraded through the crowded street in our small southern town, I felt a tinge of un-queenliness. Many others were far prettier than I, and I feared everyone was thinking it. But the tiara, long white gloves, and red roses disguised my indefinable insecurity, just as Cover Girl concealed my blemishes. Because my sisters before me had also received the honor, I felt it was another expectation for me, not a real triumph of my own. I reveled in the drama of the occasion nonetheless. It was dreamlike, and I didn't want to wake up.

The most humbling of all these senior year distinctions, however, was being voted Best All-Around by my peers. Though my résumé shined in those sweet, fanciful years, I still had a shaky infrastructure. In spite of all the affirmation and glory, my lonely soul longed for a different kind of contentment. Looking back, I was like a well-built house that had termites working underneath. Nothing seemed to convince me I was genuinely good because at my invisible core, I feared I was not.

Down the Aisle

In my second year of college, I married my handsome high school sweetheart. We had great plans and dreams. I wholeheartedly embraced the role that came with my changed status. But who was I really? The new name, preceded by "Mrs.," was a source of proud excitement at first, but eventually the dull discomfort resurfaced. We all enter marriage with bruises and secrets, and we carry our hurts with us down the aisle. I unknowingly brought my emotional baggage with me along with my sweaters, shoes, and jewelry. So I coped with the mixed bag of expectations, which comes with most marriages, by keeping threatening thoughts to myself.

In my idealistic premarital motivations, my heart's deepest desire was to be a perfect wife. I believed "becoming one flesh" simply meant combining the emotions, families, beliefs, experiences, and expectations of two fleshes, like dumping ingredients for a cake from two bowls into one. What I underestimated was the complexity of the union. I wasn't the only one carrying excess cargo.

Though our vows united us at first, soon our paths diverged. My young husband was trying to enter medical school after only three years of college. We were much in love, but he needed to focus on the difficult road ahead of him. I wanted his heart, and I wanted to give him mine, to lose my soul in him and find permanent fulfillment and joy. I never knew his own buried wounds sealed his heart, making him unavailable to relate with the intimacy I longed for. Our lives began to creep silently apart.

In search of marital bliss, I gave, surrendered, submitted, and gave some more. My naïveté expected each act of giving to yield a positive dividend from my beloved. Taking the "for better or worse" clause in our wedding vows seriously, I was committed to a lifelong happily-ever-after. I dug in my heels, determined to turn any worse into a better. Fervently believing my new focus would satisfy my earlier yearnings, I loved with dogged effort.

As time wore on, I became aware that my love-giving was searching for reciprocal benefit. I now see it was conditional love. I hadn't learned 1 Corinthians 13, which defines pure love. Though it was unfair (and humanly impossible), I expected my husband to fulfill all my needs. But he didn't even know I had any! I was, after all, a master at hiding them.

He was consumed with his work's exacting demands and never noticed I had taken a reluctant second-place seat. When nothing I did appeared impressive enough to win his attention, I reasoned the problem resided within me. *I must be insignificant. Dull.* I stayed unhealthily hushed, even as rumbles were erupting from my dungeon. Any attempts to share my feelings seemed to be irritating interruptions. He had tunnel vision, and I was outside the tunnel.

My polite, southern, churched upbringing convinced me I should not disclose any evidence of, or talk about, a struggling marriage, and its subculture didn't allow anger. My steadfastness increased.

Secret Disposal

As a young student nurse, I saw a child admitted to the emergency room who had consumed a dangerous substance. The doctors pumped out her stomach to rid her body of the toxic ingestion, then did a lab analysis to determine the poison's contents. That incident struck me. I wanted my soul to be disinfected like that child's stomach. However, I wanted no lab analysis, witnesses, records, accountability, or identification—only riddance. No ownership or connection.

We all have ghosts from seasons past we'd like to pump out and discard. For one it may be a long-ago abortion, while for others it could be experimenting with drugs, shameful associations, past promiscuity, or sex out of wedlock. We may also be embarrassed by former language or behavior—even thoughts.

Receiving Gifts

After three heart-wrenching miscarriages, the second part of my childhood dream became a reality with the birth of our first baby. But my maternal bliss was marred when my husband was too preoccupied by his work to visit me on my first day of motherhood. After weeping privately in my hospital room, I collected my emotions and strengthened my resolve to be an ideal mother and to win my hard-working husband's respect by quietly keeping on. He didn't know of his neglect's damaging effects until many years later.

Arriving home with my long awaited newborn, I settled into the satisfying experience of loving and being loved by a child. Two more gifts arrived in the next few years, and the old ache was allayed. I felt worthy as a mom. Motherhood fit me, and I loved wearing it.

However, successfully juggling the effects of my husband's stressful surgical residency, work, marriage, and raising three children on a pauper's budget was tricky. Adding housework, yard work, volunteer work, bills, church service, and children's activities required even more dexterity. It left me, as it leaves most, dizzy. Too busy in the moment to confront my ill-defined past, I never evaluated my emotions. I continued at the same pace on my personal merry-go-round. When I first heard that a definition of insanity is continuing to do the same thing while expecting a different result, I seriously questioned my sanity, but I saw no visible exit to my ongoing cycle. Confrontation felt too risky. I was inexperienced and uncomfortable with conflict.

Any unhappiness my family suffered became my responsibility. When my husband was discontented, I accepted the blame, fearing it reflected my deficiency—not nice, smart, clever, or productive enough. Good performance turned into both an obsession and a counterfeit solution. I continued to make the crippling mistake of thinking I alone could right whatever was wrong with my husband, my children, and me. However, a savior, fixer, magician, or superwoman I was not. I wore my sense of failure like silk long johns—out of sight and just underneath the outer layer.

The Truth Is...

Reality stung. My marriage was not ideal, nor was I the perfect, adored wife I had envisioned. With each disappointment, I cranked up the level of my performance another notch. However, what began as sweet intentions over time turned sour. My hushed determination to compensate for unfulfilled needs bred resentment, but since anger wasn't allowed, or even identified, it presented itself as sadness.

My husband, though well trained in his chosen profession, was untrained in matters of the heart. Mine was breaking. I had expected him to fill the void in my soul dutifully, willingly, and completely, even happily—I wanted a savior. The expectations I placed on him were burdens God never intended him to carry. Because He longs for us, God created us to feel incomplete without Him. Instead of looking to God to fill that need, I turned to my husband when the only thing that could have filled that need completely was God. That empty space remained a gaping hole, a bottomless pit. My soul grew lonelier.

A poor comprehension of biblical wifely submission encouraged my reserve, to the point of withdrawal, but I had it all wrong. I believed I was supposed to stay on (his) course quietly, suppressing my deepest sentiments—*Why do other wives receive praise for doing less than I do?*—if necessary.

As I had done with earlier relationships, I unknowingly linked my soul's well-being to my beloved's behavior. I gradually accepted his (assumedly negative) opinion of me as the truth rather than looking to God for my identity. Resentment began a knot in my stomach. I didn't understand that the biblical instructions to husbands and wives about respect and love are for *joint* strength and *mutual* benefit.

I now understand that submission means for each person to give the best he has, in the position he fills, to the marriage. By each presenting himself or herself freely and unselfishly—his or her finest efforts and natural gifts—the union's strength grows. Each position has significant value because each person is individually valuable.

But since my finest efforts seemingly had not been esteemed or even noticed, my self-worth dwindled and my position appeared insignificant. I felt unsafe, sabotaged, as if the territory around my heart had been invaded. My submission had been tossed aside, appearing valueless. I tightened my borders and beefed up my defenses.

I wish I had understood earlier the depth of the intimacy of marriage and the risk of vulnerability. When each exposes his or her deepest emotions to the other in love, the bond strengthens and mutual trust grows. There will always be disappointment and pain, because we live in a fallen world and marriage is a relationship between imperfect people. Love is unsafe by nature, for there can be no hurt without it, without feeling or affection. The stakes are high and there is always the risk of rejection—nowhere more than in marriage. But the journey is enriched by the very things that, if violated, cause the hurt—love, devotion, trust, and loyalty. Intimacy. Giving one's self away. I was unprepared—unsure of who I really was.

I had gone from striving to be a benchmark daughter, student, and leader to striving to be my husband's dream wife. I didn't see the God-me, the unique person He created me to be. Handicapped by the darkness, I subdued the very essence of my being. Prior blows guided me to hedge my honest emotions, opinions, beliefs, even desires. However, by holding back these individual components, I actually weakened our whole. But without a secure identity, they weren't really mine to give.

I wanted my beloved to embrace all of the less-than-perfect me and still reassure me I was lovable. However, I believed I disappointed him, and the thought of failing as a wife was intolerable. Interestingly, prior to marriage I was voted a winner but privately questioned my entitlement to the honors. In marriage, however, where I perceived rejection, I intuitively thought honor was deserved.

There is no other relationship like marriage and that is why Paul called it a mystery (see Eph. 5:31-32). In his letter to the Ephesians, he says that the mystery of marriage refers to Christ and the church. Surely, he is referring to the intimacy, the longing, and the vulnerability required between a man and a woman in marriage and the pain of rejection when there is less than total devotion, honesty, and complete love. Any breach hurts. Love carries a high price. God is calling us to a costly love, to be His committed bride, and marriage is the mirror, in a tiny way, of the relationship He desires to have with us. But I didn't understand then. All I knew was that my wifely rights, or expectations, didn't seem to coincide easily with God's word. I fervently believed I was following the "rules," but I was not getting the expected outcome. *This isn't fair.*

Feeling I was being denied that which (I thought) was deserved, I now see, lured me onto a rocky path, for I believed committed Christians should give up the right to themselves, submitting themselves fully to Jesus. My earthly marriage colored the picture of Christ and His bride, yet I wanted to surrender my will to God. Now, with a better understanding of my relationship to God, I know I actually *deserve* nothing—like a young child in his parents' home—everything (good) I have is by God's grace, not by my might or merit. But, believing my (wifely) rights were being violated rocked my fairness equilibrium. The imbalance made it hard to stay on course.

We all want (and need) physical arms to hold us, even when we know that only the invisible God can sustain us.

Cover-up

In search of relief, I immersed myself even further into mothering, where I felt loved and secure. It would take a searchlight probing into the darkest closet of my soul to illuminate my heartsickness and a long-handled probe to dislodge the rusted knot of fear. However, to gain wholeness, I needed to face upsetting realities and loosen my grip on past patterns.

I didn't know that my own moral excellence would delay surrender. Good behavior often camouflages our sinfulness, hiding our need for God behind our curtain of self-righteousness. In addition to being a guidepost for living, the law, or Ten Commandments, was given to expose our sins and show our need for help.

The Pharisees devoutly held to the law but didn't accept Jesus. Their meticulous law-keeping focused their eyes on themselves rather than on the One who would accomplish what could save them. Jesus called them a "brood of vipers" (Matt. 3:7), "whitewashed tombs" (Matt. 23:27), and "hypocrites" (Matt. 23:29). Their religion emphasized the outer appearance of their rituals, but their hearts concealed their wickedness. Their religious good kept them from the Best.

I feared I was a young Pharisee, proudly trying to follow, even exceed, the letter of the law. Obedient to the outer, visible world, I nonetheless lived a compromised life because I wouldn't sacrifice my appearance of success to be spiritually whole. I wanted a resurrection without a crucifixion. A secret rescuer. Self-pity, sadness, and blame came easier than self-confrontation. My faith remained in the shallows. I was wary of wading any deeper.

The carousel spun round and round, and I rode up and down on my hobbyhorse as life's music played on. The amusement park, my world, was lively and crowded with distracting sideshows. I still was convinced that if I was very, very good—at being a wife, mother, and everything else—my works eventually would redeem me. God would honor my quiet submission, thinking it was always out of love, not fear. He would credit my dutifully suppressed emotions to my heavenly tab. Ultimately, my lifelong feeling of not-quite-good-enough-ness would float away and I would feel deeply loved.

But I couldn't single-handedly secure my marriage any more than I could magically "poof" away my past misconceptions. My heart continued seeking its home, its resting place.

Chapter 3

TICK ... TOCK ...
TICK ... TOCK

He will give you the desires of your heart.

—Ps. 37:4

HAVING DEVOTED MANY wholehearted years, efforts, and emotions to nest building, my empty one left me stripped of many feathers I routinely had worn. Our children grew healthy wings and flew away. I wanted to re-feather my nest, refuel my spirit, and flap my wings, too, but I needed to rearrange my heart.

There were fewer distractions. Vacant rooms. Less laundry.

Loneliness reappeared like an old down-and-out friend from the past. Since my children largely had defined me, in their absence I needed a new definition. My life's purpose and focus were changing. With carpools, ballgames, and sleepovers no longer filling my agenda, my job description was up for reassignment. It was a new season, and I saw a fork in the road ahead. Three of my reasons for maintaining a semblance of harmony had departed.

Long Ago Seed Planting

I remember riding with my daddy as a young girl in the rural countryside of eastern North Carolina. Tobacco country. Cotton. Corn. Piled in a station wagon with sisters and cousins (before seatbelt laws), we visited Dad's Uncle Pate and Aunt Olivia on their farm. Fields of crops lined the roads on both sides as far as I could see from the car window. It seemed a long ride to reach their house.

They were waiting in the yard when we arrived on that summer morning. Pate was a quiet, gentle man. Olivia, leathery and worn, wore her white hair piled atop her head and a yellow apron tied around her waist. Their plain red brick house bespoke a world I knew nothing about. I wandered through the rooms, peering into each. In the sparse living room, I noticed Aunt Olivia's sewing basket beside a rocker. Little spheres of yarn spilled over like snowballs prepared for a wintry free-for-all. I remember a faded, patchwork quilt on an iron bed in her bedroom and I delighted to sink into its soft feather mattress. Sheer curtains danced in the light breeze that blew through an open window. A jar full of flowers and a colorful assortment of vegetables looked at home on a chipped, enamel-topped table in the kitchen. Olivia gave Daddy a brown paper bag full of pecans she had shelled and picked herself.

After lunch, we children ventured out to explore the unknown territory while the grown-ups sat on a glider in the shade and talked. At my older cousin's dare, I waved something bright to get the attention of a bull in a nearby field. I was excited when the bull turned, lowered his head, and looked aggressive. In my imagination, he charged at me and I barely escaped.

An old barn next to the field intrigued us to explore its unfamiliar contents. I discovered an array of tools I had never seen before, and bulky harnesses, dangling from big, rusted nails, decorated the walls. Old tires were stacked like Life Savers in a corner behind the hay, next to barrels big enough to hold three of us.

Dad and Pate found us in the barn, and Pate offered us a chance to milk Bessie, his brown and white cow. He pretended to spray us as we gathered close for the adventure. One by one, we squatted on an old stool beside Bessie, taking turns and giggling with each squeeze and squirt of her udder. I was mesmerized as I watched the pail fill with the white liquid I previously had seen only in the milkman's jar.

The shadow of a nearby spreading oak exuded a welcoming ambiance, and the breeze rustling its leaves cooled my hot skin as I joined the adults later that afternoon. The tree's large trunk lured me, and with a lift from Daddy, I reached a lower limb and climbed high enough to survey the layout and spot the others. But I descended just as quickly when Aunt Olivia appeared with a tray of cookies and cold milk.

Riding home at the end of the day, I imagined myself gathering eggs from the henhouse, picking vegetables from the garden, and cutting flowers for my own kitchen table before falling to sleep on the front seat beside Daddy. It was a storybook day and I had glimpsed a world I wanted to revisit.

My Garden of Eden

In those days, Daddy grew roses in a small, cultivated plot beside the fishpond at our house. Every spring he planted a few veggies and added summer annuals to his patch. He was happy in his garden. As a child, I loved sharing his after-work time with him, especially if we were alone. He let me do a little digging myself, and he encouraged me to plant seeds. Carrots were my favorite because the green growth above the ground signified a surprise waiting beneath the surface. I thrilled at each blooming zinnia and marigold, my choice of flowers.

All was well when I was with Daddy in his garden. I felt secure.

My mind's eye captured and recorded those images. An impression of peaceful country life remained tucked away in my inner journal, like undeveloped film in a canister.

Developing Pictures, Creating an Album

Over the years, my childhood memories resurfaced and my infatuation with country living grew. My passion to garden, much like my childhood yearning to mother my dolls, embodied a deep desire, not just a fleeting whim. Retrieving those stored images, I developed the pictures. A garden business was one of them.

After twenty years of in-town living, I convinced my husband to move our empty nest to a farm where I could actualize yet another dream. It was time to downsize—at least our house—for our next chapter of life.

We relocated more than ten years ago, and it was the dawning of a new season. Looking back, I believe God called me apart for a divine appointment with Him. Designing our house, getting it built, and moving was a colossal ordeal. But it was peanuts compared to the sojourn I was about to take with Jesus.

Chapter 4

AMAZING GRACE: NOW I SEE

My grace is sufficient for you.

—2 Cor. 12:9

WITH A WEARY heart and my children gone, I knew I needed to confront myself—or at least my faulty, underlying assumptions. The confusion about who, or what, lay dormant at my core still remained. Though life gratified me in so many ways, an abyss filled my innermost fiber. Hair-like triggers, sensitive to the slightest touch, lined that hidden hollow, like nerve endings scarcely under the skin's surface. Any harsh word, neglect, or criticism from my husband was magnified and crushing.

Building our new house turned from a dream into a nightmare. Both of us frustrated and overworked, we butted heads like curly horned mountain sheep. My horns chipped and finally broke. I was tired of clashing.

My feelings were raw as I descended to the deepest valley. Yet I desperately desired to draw close to my heavenly Father, whom I believed was the Someone who heard the long-ago little girl in the woods. I wanted that simple assurance I felt with Him back then. Perhaps over the years I unconsciously feared that an intimate reconnection would require exposure and, ultimately, judgment. More importantly, I suspected if I let Jesus too far inside the border, He might not like what He found. I might be asked to surrender the tiara.

Eventually my solitary despair exceeded my fear, and I was fraught to know that I was valuable and loved. My attempts at faultlessness had not captured the adoration or worth I chased, but I had nothing left to try. My internal batteries were drained and the meter was teetering near empty.

On a lonely winter evening, in an unoccupied room upstairs, I leaned against a wall as I cried out to God, "What have I done wrong? Where can I go? What else can I do? I need You. Help me! Please! I can't do this anymore." Tears spilled from my swelling eyes and dripped like a leaky faucet onto the floor. My throat tightened as if I was being strangled. I groped to breathe. My heart pounded and it seemed my chest would explode. Though the source of my desperation was not physical, I wondered if I was having a heart attack.

The noise of the TV downstairs drowned out the gasps and wails of my uncontrollable sobs. My knees grew weak and I slid down the wall and sat for what seemed like hours before finally falling asleep in a hump on the carpet. Sometime during the night, I fumbled to a bed and slept until dawn. Arising early, I quietly slipped out of bed and, kneeling, resubmitted myself to God, asking Him to walk with me back through the past and escort me into the future.

Still in my slept-in, crumpled clothes, I grabbed a warm coat, scarf, and gloves and headed outside and we drifted through the woods around the farm. He jogged my memory as He clarified my grief.

My dad's earlier death had draped a veil over my heart. The trapped sorrow necessitated action if the ache was to be relieved. Attempting to identify the anguish began a new healing process.

With holy guidance, I peered into the long-neglected cell and discovered deceit, self-pity, and pride. Surprisingly, anger hid there as well. Unuttered groans in the pit of my soul searched for free expression, like early tremors of an earthquake. My personal Richter scale was on full alert. As I descended, I began to reclaim my faith. Humbled, I asked God to show me myself, to interpret the tremors for me, and to help me make a new start. I needed His help in identifying the reason for my inmates' long-ago imprisonment.

Those early childhood memories of shame, disappointment, and insecurity flooded my consciousness as I sat on the ground underneath a pine. It was like a submarine coming to the surface after trolling the ocean depths for years. I wanted to be found—even to be found out. My secrets had become my nemesis, trapping me in solitary confinement. I was choking on my own needs and I saw ugliness embedded in my heart.

Wanting God's diagnosis, I was ready to surface. I knew the reformation I desired must begin within me, with an honest self-appraisal. Confession. I asked Jesus to salvage whatever years, acts, and emotions He could from my past.

Decades ago when I had decided to put my faith in Jesus, I had been confused. In reality, I had been converted by my own actions, but not regenerated, which is what Jesus does. I hadn't received anything new. I wasn't truly a new creature until I recognized forgiveness, activating its power. Like a newborn infant not really living until it breathes its first breath and fills its lungs with air, when I inhaled forgiveness, a new life of grace followed. Today, forgiveness is mine, like a recently discovered birthmark, and no one ever can snatch it away.

My faith had been in my own effort to make everything OK (like my decision to believe in Jesus), not in God's ability to redeem me in His Son. As long as I tightly clutched my sins (including destructive thoughts, deeds, and perceptions), they were like poison to my soul. They slowly killed my spirit.

Mark Twain said that anger is an acid that can do more harm to the vessel in which it is stored than to anything on which it is poured. I had been storing anger for a long time and didn't even know it. Resentment corroded my inner lining. When I finally laid out my secrets, giving them all to Jesus, He exchanged them for life and freedom. Giving up the need for control, I had been found. The tiara was still mine, but the need to have it was not. By letting go of my fears and exposing them, I freed a hand that could hold onto the outstretched one from my Savior.

My God-seeds were finally fertilized.

As God gently revealed these truths, I recalled the swimsuit I had stolen so long ago. That secret still hovered in the cellar with all my other hide-a-ways. My sorrowful repentance and belief in God's promise of forgiveness allowed me to lay down that wrong—and many others. The list began on that day and reached all the way back to childhood—to stealing the quarter. Through hours of weeping, that morning and into the next, I slowly released my guilt. And as the confessions poured out, I basked in the blinding light of the wonder of God. I met Mercy.

That long-ago night when I yearned to be found also returned to my mind. Not only did Jesus' light expose my sins, it also clarified my deepest desire. I wanted someone to stand up for me and share the weight of my secrets and sorrow. That Someone had always been with me, I realized, like my childhood imaginary friends. Maybe it was Him I loved in the invisible playmates.

God had been waiting for me to find Him, and I did. He held the key to my uncertain identity. The searching brought the Answer, and the Answer kept me searching.

Amazing grace, how sweet the sound,
That saved a wretch like me.
I once was lost, but now am found,
Was blind but now I see.

God provided His unfathomable forgiveness and open arms of love as I remembered, identified, and handed over each grief to Him in the days and weeks that followed. His immensity overshadowed my smallness, causing pride to take a temporary leave of absence. Instead of feeling condemnation, I felt a godly sorrow. I no longer sought to hide my wretchedness, and I almost could feel grace wash over me like a gentle ocean swell. An intense desire to let go and be free of those subtle, but burdensome, shackles welled up in me. I could taste truth and freedom, and they were delicious.

Relief that I cannot describe appeared as a formless, unexpected visitor. It was as if I was extending the baton for a lifelong lap to one who could finish the race I had been running. Though exhausted and emotionally spent, I felt oddly energized. I realized it was not the external acts that condemned me, but rather the secrecy of them and the hypocrisy of wearing purity like a jacket to disguise underlying wrinkles of deceit.

Similar to sanding down layers of paint on an old table only to discover the original color hiding beneath, I uncovered the original me for the first time. And being found for who I was brought a mixture of humiliation and delight. The humiliation, though painful, softened my heart. The delight was indescribable.

Unwilling to allow the peace of godly humility to linger, Pride slipped back into full-time patrol, ever stalking the halls of my soul. Sneaking around incognito, he wears a different outfit every day, trying to disguise my real need. Because the door he guards will not allow Jesus access, I routinely search for him in my trenches. However, under the protection of God's grace, I now am able to expose my own culpability, rather than look for vindication and a place to lay blame. My veneer has been removed, my secrets released, and my spirit freed.

I often go back to Paul's confession to the Romans in chapter seven and see that I still do much that I don't want to do. But like Paul, I know my only hope is Jesus. Nothing really good in me exists without God. What He did on the cross was for me. Believing Him is the anti-venom for my anger and regrets. I am awakening to a new dawn. Jesus left the radiance of heaven to walk through the cold, shameful darkness with me. The realization of that is sinking in.

My faith gradually oozed down from its inception. It seeped through my soul, and is now comfortably lodging in my spirit. The process is ongoing, like breathing. It never stops. I am marinating in God's love. Soaking up His forgiveness, I lay down my holdings daily and release myself. The God-seedlings in my soul garden are strong.

Chapter 5

LOOK AGAIN:
A NEW PERSPECTIVE

"There is hope for your future," declares the Lord.
                                              —Jer. 31:17

THOUGH I MISSED the activity and daily camaraderie of my old neighborhood, I fell in love with my new home, aptly named Cowlick Farm for the cowlicks each of my children possess. I melted in the serenity of the country.

Enthralled by the noises of the critters, great and small, I was carried back in time to some of the best memories of my childhood. Nostalgic fragrances of honeysuckle and ligustrum's faint intangible presence evoked sweet reminiscences of summer nights playing kick the can. In the mornings, I watched birds industriously prepare their nests, lay their eggs, and patiently wait. And weeks later, from my nest-side seat, I eyed the newborns begging for food with gaping beaks.

Many a summer dusk, I was privileged to observe deer feeding and foxes hunting. After sunset, the songs and croaks of bullfrogs, crickets, locusts, and other members of a nocturnal choir lulled me. I was entertained by the symphony of noise in an auditorium of dark silence—nature's melodies.

An idyllic peace settled around me, like my grandmother's snuggly shawl, when I watched from a rocker on the porch as my old mare grazed in her pasture. What fun it was to slip on my red wellies, while still in my nightgown, and walk to the barn in the tranquility of early morning. I relished the earthy smell of hay combined with the steamy, hearty aroma of my first cup of coffee. My senses tweaked and enlivened, as if being stimulated for the first time. Surrounded by the natural, I learned to appreciate things I previously had overlooked.

On this farm, I felt connected to God, as if He were texting messages to my heart. My "me-ness" was changing to "Him-ness" as the design of His world transposed my worldliness. Hearing noises from the wild without seeing the source became a sweet reassurance that there were angels all around, like bodyguards in the unseen. I acquired new companions with wings, claws, snouts, and hooves. My fraught soul began to relax. I yearned to surrender to the comfortable new place where I felt lovingly embraced. A giant step closer to peace, my understanding of life broadened. I was entering into a deeper relationship with Jesus through His creation.

So You Want to Grow Flowers?

> In repentance and rest you will be saved,
> In quietness and trust is your strength.
>
> —Is. 30:15

Shortly after moving, I was ready to embark on my new adventure and eager to learn the business of market gardening. However, my Lord appeared with another plan. He wanted to teach me the business of heaven. Through His very creation—the dirt, seeds, weeds, and flowers—He revealed the gospel.

I thought my gardening endeavor was to be about me growing flowers, but I was wrong. It was about God growing me. By answering my long-standing prayers for wisdom and redemption, He was setting me free. From learning to drive a tractor to harvesting and selling the flowers, I felt the Lord beside me, offering a poignant lesson in every detail.

I met with Jesus daily in my overalls. He knelt with me in the dirt. Through it all, He displayed His great love, perfect provision, and divine plan. Many "aha" moments occurred where the complex meaning of biblical words became as plain as day, as real as dirt, and as present as the air I breathed.

My Garden, My Life

My visions of growing exact replicas of flowers from catalogs I had perused in January often were met with a struggle to bridge the gap between what I hoped for and the disappointing results. This became an apt depiction of my life, of me not being the person I wanted to be—like my enthusiastic plan to be a perfect wife and the disillusionment I felt when I was not.

Embracing the less-than-perfect reality of the present helps me let go of the past. I am learning to grow where I am planted, like the flower seeds. Far from springing to quick perfection, my garden is a work in progress, as am I. Every day presents a different challenge with unique needs. The work never will be finished—in the garden or in me. It will continue as long as there is life. My work on the farm proves the need to balance strenuous physical work with a heart that rests in God. I cannot manage alone. This truth both humbles and gratifies me, for I am far wiser for having begun the challenge.

Seeing the Extraordinary in the Ordinary

I go to prepare a place for you.

—John 14:2

The stories that follow illustrate the ways God revealed Himself to me, prepared a path, and led me to that night of confession and subsequent renewal. Some of the revelations were new insights at the time. Many others gave physical form to what I already knew as God named, identified, or clarified previously vague concepts.

In preparing the flower field for cultivation, I faced myself and cried out to God to cultivate me. Creating a garden opened the gate to my spirit. God used simple metaphors to explain life's inevitable ups and downs. Through this process, He unlocked my cellar and stepped into my private world. He plowed my dormant field, planted holy seeds, and fertilized them with His very presence.

I continue to see Him in the everyday occurrences of life, on and off the farm. Even as I write this, more parallels from the garden arise, which continue to affirm my faith.

For some of these experiences, my interpretation is different now than it was at the time and becomes clearer with each word I write. It is difficult to distinguish precisely when each revelation took place. They are like the flowers I collect in a basket. How would I remember the order in which each was picked?

God has been cultivating a crop from seeds He planted in me for a lifetime. I witnessed a prolific harvest, and I want to share the fruit.

Mine has been a good life, perhaps even enviable to some, and it gets richer with each insight. God continues to refocus my attention from myself to Him. Now I want Him to have all the glory. I want to be but an individual reflection of Him. No earthly titles or tiaras are necessary. It is the eternal crown of glory I desire (see 1 Peter 5:4).

GLORIOUS OVERALLS:
GOD'S GLORY IS OVER ALL

Overalls are the best thing to wear in the garden. They don't pull or pinch around the waist (depending on my addicted-to-chocolate intake the day before). They eradicate pesky mid-body gaps in clothing where dirt or unwanted, biting, skin-attaching critters can gain entrance. Best of all, they eliminate constraints when reaching, pulling, digging, kneeling, or performing any other exercise that typically occurs while gardening.

If you wear them loose enough, they accommodate stomach swells resulting from too many snacks consumed during breaks or lunches gulped in haste. There are no constricting buttons to release. The large pockets work for holding gloves, clippers, hankies, lip balm, cell phone, Life Savers, sunscreen, and a myriad of other things *needed* while gardening.

So accustomed to wearing overalls, I forget they aren't the norm for a graying, fifty-something mom to wear on a regular basis. I've received many a stare and comment from strangers and friends alike while standing in the register line wearing my dirty overalls. Invariably, strangers inquire, creating an opening to pass on a garden miracle.

But God doesn't care as much about my external garb as my internal attire. It has added to my pleasure to think that He, the God of all things great and small, met me so faithfully, consistently, and lovingly, and showed Himself to me so clearly while I was tired, dirty, and usually wearing overalls.

Chapter 6

MOVING AND
BEING MOVED

---

*Then Abram moved his tent and came and dwelt by
the oaks… and there he built an alter to the Lord.*

—Gen. 13:18

Thirty Years Ago

ARRIVING IN AN unfamiliar town two thousand miles away from your previous home is a challenge. Add to that three small children—ages five, three, and nine months—and you have an adventure. A three-year-old Springer Spaniel was the sixth member of our young family. We were returning to North Carolina, our home state, from Utah, where my husband had been in a surgical residency for five years. He would join us three weeks later.

A lot of searching, both external and internal, led us to choose a small community twenty-five miles from the town where we grew up. Our new-to-us, but very old, wooden clapboard house was bigger than our previous four dwellings combined. Every room displayed a fireplace, and the ceilings reached more than ten feet. A delightful *To Kill a Mockingbird*-type screened porch at the back door slanted ever so slightly, leaning away from the house. The foundation had sunken over its many years, and my little boys found the slight tilt custom-made for rolling trucks, marbles, and Matchbox cars. Everything that had wheels ended up on the low side by the end of the day. We would spend the next twenty years repairing, rearranging, and renovating this old classic.

On our second day in this empty echo-filled house, I found several ripe tomatoes perched on the ledge of the leaning screened porch, like little treasures just waiting to be discovered. Shortly after, the neighbor across the street, Bernard, appeared and introduced himself as the elusive bearer of tomatoes and other recent kindnesses. We were all amused to put a face to the mystery deliverer. He was slight of size and hunched in posture, but large in character—a perfect model for a Norman Rockwell painting. His easy, toothy smile and slightly protruding ears framed the crook in his pointy nose.

A natural with kids, he established our camaraderie as he talked lovingly with them. When he gently picked up my crawling toddler, who cried and needed a diaper change, our friendship was sealed. He had a tender heart for little ones, and my three quickly became devoted to him. He checked on us daily and regularly left calling cards of produce from his garden or specialties from his kitchen. Sweet potato pies were a favorite.

Bernard became more like a beloved uncle than a kind neighbor. He freely advised and disagreed with each of us. Though he often was cantankerous, we welcomed his gentle-as-a-lamb presence into our lives. He won our hearts. So after twenty years of neighboring, he didn't take kindly to our decision to move four miles out of town.

Nevertheless, I was lured to the country as surely as my husband had wooed me in the halls of Rose High School. The dormant idea of living on a farm, working in a field, and growing and selling flowers finally had germinated into the dream of a romantic adventure.

Keeping a fatherly eye on us was no longer convenient, but Bernard managed to stay in close touch when we left. Being a part-time farmer himself, he felt comfortable in our new space and became a regular overseer of our house-building and farm-renovation project. Sometimes he graded my decisions rather critically. I either worried him by my ignorance or annoyed him with my methods, but he remained a committed friend. I only occasionally received a compliment, but I always felt his love.

In hindsight, I see how God positioned Himself through Bernard to advise, accompany, and love me as I began my garden journey. He helped bridge the uncertain gap between the comfortable life I left and the new unknown. Our charming, pre-Civil War house on historic Main Street differed vastly from our simple new home on a farm. At the time, I had no idea that the physical move to the country was the beginning of a spiritual move in my heart.

I Considered My Field

She considers a field and buys it.

—Prov. 31:16

A week after our move, all our furniture found a place in our new house, yet partially unpacked boxes still crowded every room. Piles of "undecideds" crammed the corners, while the cupboards and closets quickly filled with "for sures."

But before the paint had dried or the pictures were hung, I began to select the location for my garden. I gathered pertinent material and studied books and websites about growing for market. After carefully surveying the farm's layout, I decided on a field near the house. It had been cultivated previously and wouldn't require any tree clearing or ground leveling.

The field was convenient to both the house and the existing tobacco barn I planned to refurbish into a garden retreat. In my enthusiasm, I mistakenly thought it would be a practical, workable size (a modest two acres!). Additionally, the former farmer had described the soil in that field as very fertile, encouraging me, a budding flower grower.

In considering the field, I analyzed the shade the tall pine trees on the perimeter might produce. Would the shade block necessary sunshine or would it provide needed relief from the harsh rays? I took into account the field's rectangular shape and its topography as I mentally designed the garden, positioning the rows just right. Even more questions filled my mind. How well would it drain after a storm? How would it look beside the long, narrow lane entering Cowlick Farm? Would it be an attractive asset or a messy distraction?

Though I desired a pretty garden, I kept my original intention in mind and tried to be practical, fighting the temptation to arrange it for visitor approval. Pushing pride aside, I finally designed the garden for production purposes only, not beauty. It was a business garden after all.

I Considered My Soul

I was fatigued from adjusting my hats of designer, contractor, painter, decorator, wife, and now, flower grower. In all the activity, I had taken little time to be quiet with God. However, even with my preoccupations, I became subtly aware of the personal analogies regarding the field for my new garden. Everything I pondered became applicable to renovating my soul's dormant field.

I began to see my worship time as a field to cultivate. My inner self—my "soul field"—needed spiritual nourishment just as my body needed food. I exercised daily, and I definitely ate more than enough food for energy and sustenance, yet I didn't pay sufficient attention to my spiritual condition. My soul was hungry, and the inmates grew restless.

I sensed God calling me, but I put Him on the back burner to simmer. Though I had been a practicing, professing Christian for many years, I was beginning to realize that my faith was like the veneer on a piece of furniture, a thin covering that had appeared shiny and clean but was not deep enough to sustain the life I wanted. I again remembered Jesus' rebukes to the Pharisees. His words to them were harsher than to any other group. My veneer, fearfully, began to appear pharisaical.

Though I had sensed a supernatural presence in the early process of moving and gardening, the physical requirements of my new endeavor distracted me.

But before the end of that first year, I probed uncomfortably deep. I began questioning how I had been communicating with God. If my private worship place was not easily accessible, I wouldn't go and meet with my Father. Life was too busy, and unless I intentionally made room for God in my daily agenda, He got squeezed out. I could feel that some part of me was shriveling up, like unused muscles. The time had come to move God to the front burner and turn up the heat. My spiritual quads needed stretching.

Just as I planned for my garden to be conveniently close to my house, I began thinking about the convenience of my personal worship. If my garden had been farther away, I would have made fewer trips there in the heat of the day. I may have postponed going there at all. Likewise, I often relegated my time with God to the end of the day when I was tired and ready for bed, trusting He was kind enough to understand.

As I had considered level ground and tree clearance in my chosen flower field, I began to see that God was clearing my heart of obstacles and leveling my inner ground for construction. He was building the quiet place of my soul in hopes of residing there, furnishing it with love, and providing a safe place for my spirit. But still not grasping His full intention, I continued to think horizontally, glancing at the world around me for affirmation and value, with a mindset mostly about me. I sensed that more was happening than I could see with my physical eyes. I was morphing, but into what?

I widened the dragnet in my soul search. How could I position myself to receive "Sonshine" and sufficient shade for rest? What trees in my life blocked the Son? How well did I drain after storms in my life? The questions bombarded me day and night. My spirit disquieted, it felt like I was waiting for a new baby to be born. New life was imminent, but the exact time, place, and appearance was yet to be seen. Labor pains lingered while my spirit's contractions continued.

Though my desire for honesty and disclosure grew, I didn't pursue them aggressively. I remained a spectator. I wanted to restore order to my unhinged life, but I didn't know how. I couldn't see past the demanding flower-grower's "to-do" list before me. I sensed God was drawing me closer, but I didn't realize how close He already was.

Looking back, His light was shining as bright as the July sun, but I added a spiritual UV lens to my physical sunglasses to lessen the intensity of both. I chose to remain in my comfort zone, a dimly lit place where not all was exposed.

That night when, at the end of my rope, I had asked Jesus to rescue me, inviting Him further inside, began a new relationship with God. I crossed the threshold into a different zone. He encouraged me to be honest, preparing a secure place for me to see my heart's undistorted reflection. I needed a vigorous soul. My body was dying daily, but my spirit would live forever.

Private Lessons

Loneliness often accompanies God's voice. As my desire for fellowship with Him grew, my solitude also increased. He used the garden to distract my worldly eyes and focus them on Him. Like a shop owner closing for inventory, I took stock of my life and all that was stored on my spirit's shelves. My supply was depleted. Before reopening for business, I reordered my ambitions and purposes.

Alone with God, I surrendered into transparent vulnerability. My soil grew richer and spiritual flowers sprung up in my secret soul garden before an audience of only One. I felt safe confessing and grieving with Him.

A Scripture repeatedly came to my mind:

> When you pray, you are not to be like the hypocrites; for they love to stand and pray in the synagogues and on the street corners so that they may be seen by men. Truly I say to you, they have their reward in full. But you, when you pray, go into your inner room, close your door and pray to your Father who is in secret, and your Father who sees what is done in secret will reward you.
> —Matt. 6: 5-6

Was my inner room to be my two acres? I wondered if my garden field would be my worship place and if I would reap more than flowers there.

Our performance-geared culture tells us that doing anything good in private, without getting recognition, is anathema, even in the body of Christ. We choose to serve, but we too often want temporal credit, the all-important, all-consuming approval of others. Recalling those life-long yearnings to feel loved and approved, I sensed God's healing touch as He drew me near to Him in private. I began to feel Him loving me.

Clear Transmission

Cease striving and know that I am God.

—Ps. 46:10

I need frequent time apart from life's racket to hear my Father's quiet voice. I must have a place where I can sever all associations between my spiritual world and the noisy material life surrounding me. Not necessarily a specific, visible place, it can be anywhere I am. However, the senses often hinder, not help, my communication with Him. The constant input through my five earthly portals of entry provides too much stimulus. My mind wanders.

I must slow down my inner traffic. Putting my perceptions on hold—requiring roadblocks at all entry points—quiets my soul. In stillness I hear the music of heaven, which accompanies intimacy with God. It is like trying to find good reception on the radio—a station without static. The interference in our lives keeps us from tuning in.

Conscious New Beginning

As I increasingly sensed God's nearness, I knew we journeyed a lifelong voyage together. That was the conscious new beginning of the rest of my life. God would meet me in my overalls in the garden, away from the maddening crowd, when my soul was ready. I prepared a garden for growing flowers that would be seen, but He prepared a garden to grow me, in the unseen. After my "levy" had broken, the floodgate of confession opened and a deluge ensued. Beginning upstairs, it continued through the woods and into the garden. God rolled away the stone that hid the entrance to my soul's dungeon, releasing the fearful doubts from their hiding places.

Through the ordinary stuff of gardening, I was seeing the extraordinary, and I was changed forever. I understood John Bunyan's words from his book, *The Acceptable Sacrifice:*

> Conversion to God is not so easy and so smooth a thing as some would have men believe it is. Why is man's heart compared to fallow ground, God's Word to a plough, and his ministers to ploughmen, if the heart indeed has no need of breaking, in order to the receiving of the seed of God unto eternal life?[1]

The One who heard me, a little girl in the woods long ago, had returned to hear me in the garden. Or perhaps it was I who had come back and was now listening. My security and identity were re-routed. They now come from God, not man. I am, thankfully, able to hear and converse anywhere, any time with Him, though He often speaks in a whisper. Our relationship is established—we need no warm up or small talk.

Chapter 7

HOEING AND ROWING

For ground that ... brings forth vegetation useful to those for whose sake it is also tilled, receives a blessing from God.
—Heb. 6:7

FOR MY TWENTY-NINTH wedding anniversary, I received not a little blue box, but a shiny, red, refurbished Farmall tractor with power steering. I had wanted a convertible. What a beauty! I climbed aboard and took a five-minute impromptu driver's ed course from the refurbisher, our good friend Stan. After a successful trial trip around the barn, I was as proud as a peacock of my new set of wheels.

Donning overalls and my wide-brimmed straw hat, I officially made my debut as a bona fide tractor owner. With no small amount of satisfaction, I drove my snazzy convertible into my chosen field. On that momentous occasion, I sat erect with my head held high, as if I were being presented to an elite society. Had there been an audience, white gloves and a mechanical parade wave would have been in order. Maybe even the old tiara.

A total novice at farming, I needed a lot of help. I was, after all, a *slightly* over middle-aged empty-nester and mother of three who never had farmed, sat on a tractor, considered a field, or harvested a crop. Despite this reality, I wanted not only to sow a few seeds, but also to farm two whole acres well enough to produce bounty to sell.

Rowing

Acknowledging my lack of experience, I proceeded to learn. I read, watched, and practiced; and Bernard, who didn't hesitate to point out my mistakes, advised me. He often appeared as if from nowhere, and I'd look up from concentrating on driving in a straight line to see him watching. He'd smile, shake his head, or point his finger at me. With no more children around to divert him, my farming skills, or lack thereof, engaged all of his scrutiny. He usually left as imperceptibly as he came.

The first time I plowed the whole field, I felt like I had accomplished something akin to carving a perfect stone sculpture of George Washington. I admired the beautiful dirt I had unearthed with its large, coal black chunks and rich texture. It smelled ironically clean, like freshly cut grass. The subtle, sweet scent was one of God's gifts—unseen, yet in plain view.

For the first time in my life, I knew what Daddy had smelled when we rode in the country long ago. When I shut my eyes, I saw the faint smile on his face as he inhaled the country air of freshly plowed fields. I felt a delightful reconnection to my dad. My mind flashed back to that storybook day with him when I experienced my first inkling of a desire for farm life.

Confident that the deeper I went, the more fertile the soil would be, I plowed one way … then back the other … a little deeper … then crisscrossed … a little deeper … and back again. Boy, was I good!

Then, as nature would have it, a succession of thunderstorms drenched us. It rained and rained and rained and then—it rained some more. Our little neck of the woods even made the national weather news that spring. I considered building an ark instead of planting a field.

When it stopped, I hurried out to admire my masterpiece. Quicksand! That's what it had become. That rich, black soil mixed with April's torrential downpours had become a quagmire for the middle-aged farmer extraordinaire. With my first step, I sunk so deep, so fast that I lost my balance. My second step yielded me torso deep. Defeat! Exasperation! Humiliation!

Following a brief pity party, I worked to get my footing. Eventually, I pulled one bare foot from the field, leaving my clog to the earthworms. Then I finally tugged out the second foot, naked. To this day, a great broken-in pair of red leather clogs rests peacefully somewhere beneath the cucumber row.

My masterful bog took forever to dry up enough for me to stay above ground, let alone drive a tractor without sinking. But when it dried, I drove. I diligently spent hours learning how to "row." Finally, mission accomplished—I had successfully mounded the dirt into rows for planting my flower seeds.

No doubt about it, this time Confidence herself rode in the seat next to me. As I finished, I saw Bernard watching with a trace of a smile on his face. I knew I had earned a compliment from him for my just completed, perfectly created rows.

But his eyes said something else. *Not straight?* In disbelief, I looked back. The rows were wavy at best. I thought the slight waviness was acceptable, but soon learned that for future row tending, the rows needed to be very straight. If not, the plow point can't fit between the rows for weeding, and the tiller can't till without disrupting the row beside it. The tires will roll over the part that juts out of line. Therefore, I started over and over and over again—and again and again.

Bernard had once instructed me, "Locate an immovable object at a distance beyond the end of the row where you are heading.

Keep your eyes fixed on it, rather than looking to the right or left, while trying to drive straight." But as I plowed, I frequently had rotated around to admire my plowing.

Luke 9:62 took on new meaning for me: "No one, after putting his hand to the plow and looking back, is fit for the kingdom of God." I knew my less-than-desirable plowing skills would not deem me unfit for the kingdom, but the lesson impressed my heart. Focusing my eyes backwards, sideways, or any way but on Jesus makes life harder and my ultimate purpose more difficult to accomplish.

Learning to plow provided a visual image for spiritual lessons. My attention must be focused on forward movement. I can't spend my born-again life looking back at either my mistakes or my spiritual highs. The past is forgiven, and my earlier encounters with God, though wonderful, must not be my only testimony. Looking forward, I try to see evidence of Him daily and focus on my long-term goal: eternity. Like spotting the immovable object to make straight rows, I am learning to focus on Jesus to grow straight.

The plowing fiasco reminded me of the story of Peter in Matthew 14 when he was walking on the water to meet Jesus. After getting out of the boat, Peter fearfully turned his eyes on the wind and the turbulent waters. Seeing potential trouble, he began to sink. When he cried out for help, Jesus stretched out His hand, took hold of him, and saved him. This truth struck deep within me.

Like Peter, I want the courage to step out when Jesus calls, no matter how daunting the circumstances.

Awakening the Dead

Shortly after that lengthy and humbling row-making adventure, a variety of new, pretty growth appeared. I was thrilled to see how quickly the just-planted seeds sprouted. Being ever so optimistic and naïve, I never dreamed they were all weeds. I soon learned my extensive plowing had unearthed a multitude of dormant weed seeds. I had awakened the dead!

Weeds grew rampant, and my garden was completely green before my babies (seeds) settled into their new beds. I was shocked and unprepared for what I saw. My heart sank and eventually settled somewhere near my big toe. It was like coming home from vacation and discovering someone had broken in.

I had spent so much energy and time in vain—it actually had had the opposite effect of what I had intended. I felt like someone other than me had planted the field I had labored over. Green and beautiful from a distance, what grew was not what I had planned. I didn't know that without any plowing or planting at all, the field would yield a harvest of weedy grasses, dandelions, or buttercups. It was a picture of marriage—some of the seeds we brought into our marriage were weed seeds. They, too, sprouted and grew out of control before we identified them. Many beautiful flowers grew, but the weeds threatened their growth.

Two more lessons became clear. From afar, a green field appears pretty—its dandelions resemble lovely flowers—but a close examination reveals uneven ground and weedy grasses. The garden must go through a destructive process to become productive. In the same way, many lives look pretty from afar also, but a close-up of the inside may reveal an undesirable crop ravaged by internal storms. I recognized dandelions growing in my soul field. I was slow to find my soul's trusted Plower.

In addition, care must be taken when choosing the immovable marker for straight rowing. Quite possibly my chosen fixture wasn't as steadfast as I had thought. Similarly, there is only one Being that does not change. His name is God. A husband, wife, father, mother, or friend is not immovable. Only God is the same yesterday, today, and forever.

Waiting on God

The ground in my garden needed to be broken and re-broken for the clumps of soil to be manageable. Then I, the gardener, could choose what I wanted to plant. In addition, my diligence to plant and water determined the success of the harvests. I also learned that weeding out unwanted competition and providing needed support would increase my productivity.

As I recorded these thoughts, labors, and lessons learned, I felt nudged in my spirit again: "Don't plan without Me. I could save you much labor. Do it in My time, not yours." I retreated to my soul-garden manual, the Bible, and spent time with the Original Gardener. I snuggled in the sanctuary of an old rocking chair overlooking my field and read Ecclesiastes 3:1-2:

> There is an appointed time for everything. And there is a time for every event under heaven. ... A time to give birth and a time to die; A time to plant and a time to uproot what is planted.

(*God even knows about weeding!*) Again, I sensed this entire garden experience was about more than growing flowers, and the nudgings were personal, not gardening tips.

My search continued. "Unless the Lord builds the house, they labor in vain who build it" (Ps. 127:1). My labor often seemed fruitless, but I felt oddly reassured that I still would produce flowers. Ecclesiastes 2:22-26 says when we labor without God, we labor in vain. Indeed, in vanity we think ourselves capable of living divinely fruitful lives without heavenly help.

Sinking ... Again

Soon I realized, despite months of hard work, I had not produced the garden of my dreams, nor had I found success in many of the required tasks. My childhood dream of country life was unraveling, and I felt incapable of sustaining it. Self-doubt again flooded my consciousness. The intensity of the labor and the time required far surpassed my anticipation. A nine-to-five job sounded easy, almost lazy. Washing windows, cutting grass, and mucking horse stalls felt like leisure activity by comparison.

I privately acknowledged I had, like in my early years of marriage and motherhood, busily proceeded with my project without spending time with God. Not only were my rows not straight and my flowers outmatched by weeds, but my inexperience clearly showed. My middle-aged, hot-flashing body was the only thing that looked experienced! Had my hair been whiter and long enough to knot atop my head, I might have resembled Great-aunt Olivia. What had seemed rather romantic as a child now failed to impress.

I had the scary thought that my only perennials would be the dirt under my nails and the ache in my back. Would the wrinkles in my sun-parched skin outnumber the flowers I produced? My friends were getting manicures, playing tennis, and traveling. Some pursued challenging careers or escaped life's hectic pace through captivating novels. Others sat by a pool sipping sodas, margaritas, or fancy bottled water, having intelligent conversations with other humans. They grasped the latest headlines and were well acquainted with local goings-on

I, on the other hand, slurped water from a dirty garden hose and talked to four-legged critters, winged companions, and creepy, crawly, biting tenants. The only news apparent to me was the most recent weed or the newest rash on my skin, and the biggest gossip was what was growing in the ground.

"Everyone but me is on vacation," I whined, "and my garden doesn't allot vacation days." Time away resulted in the garden growing out of control and my frustration level rising. Self-pity knocked at my door again. Yet instead of seeing the reality—I chose to garden, and I needed to accept it—I felt ashamed of my attitude. Disheartened, I took refuge in Isaiah 40:29-31:

> He gives strength to the weary,
> And to Him who lacks might He increases power.
> Though youths grow weary and tired,
> And vigorous young men stumble badly,
> Yet those who wait for the Lord
> Will gain new strength;
> They will mount up with wings like eagles,
> They will run and not get tired,
> They will walk and not become weary.

Relieved that not only middle-aged women, but even youths, grow tired and stumble, too, I knew my strength would grow if I would wait on God. Yet I still felt dull and defeated. I didn't want to wait but wanted help right then. My silent, but very real, adversary took advantage of my impatience and accused me of failure. I believed it. Discouraged and embarrassed (though no one was watching me), I was tempted to give it all up and throw in the trowel.

Then Galatians 6:9 quietly slipped into focus:

> Let us not lose heart in doing good, for in due time we will reap
> if we do not grow weary.

I remembered what Oswald Chambers said many years ago: "All our fretting and worrying is caused by planning without God."[2]

Blessed Are the Poor in Spirit

In the quiet of my safe haven, I felt God encouraging me: "Let's garden together. I made the dirt, seeds, and sun. Trust Me to teach you. Don't give up. We're not finished yet." The temptation to quit still lurked nearby, but this inner reassurance convinced me to continue. Inspiration slowly replaced discouragement. "For My thoughts are not your thoughts, nor are your ways My ways" (Isa. 55:8). Becoming increasingly aware of my neediness, I wanted to incorporate His ways into my physical work.

I remembered a verse I learned as a child: "Trust in the Lord with all your heart and do not lean on your own understanding" (Prov. 3:5). I had relied on my own limited understanding my whole life, looking for tangible assurance in a physical world. We all possess this dangerous tendency, believing more knowledge, possessions, or effort is the answer. We think manipulating our circumstances to avoid painful realities will sustain us. Achieving, in the natural, felt more substantial to me than trusting a God I couldn't see.

A strangely beautiful thing began to happen. My worldly confidence (accomplishments and abilities) turned into humility. My spirit was finally plowed up, crumbly and manageable, and ready to be planted. Tilled and broken, I was ready to obey, and even the smallest bit of obedience from a believer opens heaven. The plowed garden perfectly depicted my weepy confession to God after the soul wrenching night of despair. I clearly saw how brokenness is a necessity for knowing God intimately.

I took a renewed look at my garden and my life. Though I still didn't comprehend the extent of my Father's teaching, I knew He reached to me in and through the dirt, labor, plans, and failures. Not a single experience wasted, I saw that my greatest field of labor was myself. First Corinthians 3:9 says, "You are God's field, God's building." I knew it would take years, if not a lifetime, to understand and discern the significance of it all.

God is stronger than my circumstances, and Romans 8:28 says He will use every situation for good for those who love Him. When I give even my soul's darkest nights to God, I find the mysterious value of darkness, which is His grace shining through. Just as the blades on my plow break through the soil's hardened upper layer, God broke open the dark place in my spirit, preparing my soul for a beautiful harvest.

He actually uses our difficulties as His plow blades to break through our crusty edges. Love and laughter are as the rain and sun. Only God knows what is required to attain His goal, which I cannot see. As I submitted my broken clods to Him, I drew closer. Peace slipped into my soul garden like morning dew.

I was excited about this first leg of my midlife trek. Though clueless about the exact destination, I was confident in Who led me. Humbled beyond words, I realized that God, my Creator, had met me, an ordinary mom and homemaker, in my overalls in the dirt. I longed to share this with those I loved, but it was to be a very quiet and personal journey, a solo expedition.

Chapter 8

SEEDS: SOWING AND GROWING

The seed is the word of God.

—Luke 8:11

VISUALIZE BEING ABANDONED immediately after birth. With no one to feed, love, hold, or teach you, you'd be all alone in a frightening world, surrounded by forces able to sweep you away in an instant. Welcome to the world of a seed.

Seeds are wonderments that continue to amaze me. Placing my first order as a new flower grower, I did not know what to expect. When the seeds arrived, I found each one's individual size, shape, and color interesting. The tiny kernels are actually dead little parts of a once alive and thriving plant.

I picked one particular seed and analyzed its birth, first home, and progression from early childhood through adolescence. At the end of a flower's natural life, its seeds fall off and not only leave the comfort of home, but also lie helpless on the ground. They are at the mercy of all creation. Storms may drench and beat them. Deer, dogs, and other neighborhood critters trample them. The sun scorches and dries them. Birds pick them up, flying the tiny seeds to foreign places to eat them. And on it goes. If a seed survives all these perils, it eventually seeks security in the ground, unless it is collected for new life in a different home.

I never before had considered the existence of a seed, its origin, planting, growth, and ultimate harvest. Impatiently, I mentally had fast-forwarded to gorgeous flowers. However, as the seasons passed, the mom in me began to look at each seed as my child. I was responsible for each special little creature. (Perhaps as an empty-nester, I relished the thought.) I officially became a foster parent, ordered my chosen seeds, and prepared beds for them.

Seeding and Feeding

Upon the seeds' arrival at their adopted home, my barn, I lovingly unpacked them and thrust them into the soil, where they found themselves abandoned once again. Instead of tucking them away for eight hours each night, I bedded them down for eight weeks, giving up all direct contact with them. I either actively pushed them into the ground or lightly raked dirt over them and left them alone, depending on the type of seed.

My little friends went through a long, lonely period, not seeing the light of day. Eventually, they lost their previous shape and identity. Mining for minerals, they searched for the soil's nourishment as they struggled to grow in their new home. Had they been human, their new existence might have disappointed them. Perhaps they believed their adoption would offer a different kind of life.

This process reminded me of my long-ago, newfound Christianity when I believed I was going to get a new life, too. Disappointment filled my heart when the "old" me resumed life as before. I, too, strived to thrive. If only I had understood who had adopted, chosen, and called me when I was born again. If only I had grasped to whom I really belonged. Royalty! I became an heir to the King but lived with a pauper's insecurity.

The seeds needed to grow roots downward before reaching upward. This first process, rooting deep into the soil, is unseen—no show, beauty, or glory. Yet the most important part of their future well-being rested in this development.

As the seeds' roots search for nutrients and water beneath the surface, they provide anchorage for the plant, preparing it for life above ground. They build muscle, like we humans strive for in a gym. I must encourage the seeds to reach deep for their sustenance. Staying close to the surface ultimately could lead to their demise.

I have noticed God frequently grows life under cover of darkness, like an embryo in the obscurity of the womb and morning dew after nights of drought. Fresh blooms greet me in the morning, but I seldom spot any at day's end. God does His creating work while I sleep, and at sunup, I remind myself, "Joy comes in the morning" (Ps. 30:5). As God's children, we can be sure we'll have periods of darkness in this life, but just as sure that He is present in our darkness.

My new seed babies finally germinated (set their anchors) and sprouted, sending up tiny shoots above ground. I still marvel that they survived their dark isolation. Significantly, by first lying dormant the seeds' growth process was set in motion even before they began their underground search.

Each stage in the seed's life cycle paralleled a stage in my personal growth. I, like the seed, experienced a dormancy—out of view and alone with God—before I began to realize my full identity. Sometimes being alone with God rather than busy in the world feels like dormancy. In my time away from people, I met with God in private and my faith rooted.

After struggling through the obscurity of the dirt, the new seedlings grow upward for two to three months. They bask in the sun before they become a pageant of brilliance. Being intricately formed and magnificently colored, the exquisite flowers look nothing like their former appearance as seeds. Resembling the developmental period from the single cell egg to the fully formed human, a seed's transformation is a miracle that is thrilling to behold. Humbly, I remembered how soaking up the Son, Jesus, anchored my root system, allowed my inmates to escape, and prepared me to sprout.

Though on the exterior the flower doesn't resemble the seed, the plant gains all it needs from the tiny seed. Every seed possesses tremendous potential, merely waiting for the opportunity to grow. Each kernel has stored within it a small amount of energy, which it needs when germinating to push through its hard outer coating to the soil and sunlight. If I plant it too deep or allow the soil to become hard, then the seed may be defeated before it even makes its debut. I, then, become responsible for its death. I am confident when planting that every seed has all it requires within itself to become like its parent. Jesus' words are the same as the seeds, containing all I need to grow into His image.

Though knowing God's Word is important, it can bring new life only as it becomes an integral part of who I am. James exhorts, "Receive the word implanted, which is able to save your souls" (James 1:21). The Word becomes implanted in me as I spend time in it just like the seed needs time in the ground to draw its strength.

When I seek the world's sustenance, my satisfaction becomes superficial, and my heart, ultimately, unfulfilled. If my security lies in my worldly accomplishments, possessions, performance, or other people, I am in grave danger should these things suddenly fail or be taken away.

Interestingly, we see huge deciduous trees uprooted in heavy storms because, though large and widespread, their root systems are relatively shallow. Pine trees, however, have very deep taproots and, while frequently broken, they seldom uproot. Following God takes a deep, inner search for truth, like the underground journey in the life of a seed. Jesus said, "I am the way, and the truth, and the life" (John 14:6). Only through Him can we get to God. I have repeatedly asked, "What is my anchor? From where do I draw my strength?"

Rooty and Fruity

Flower seeds require heat to germinate. Since I don't have the aid of a heated greenhouse, I must wait for the ground temperature in my garden to rise before planting my seeds in the soil. Similarly, after God plants a seed in us, He allows our lives to "heat up" in order for the seed to germinate. He will use difficult circumstances to strengthen our moral fiber. Heat is a requirement for growing flowers—and souls. For maximum strength and full maturity, adversity must come.

Whatever lives within me influences me. Like the seed in the ground, we are exhorted to "Let the word of Christ richly dwell within you" (Col. 3:16). However, dwelling with God can be problematic, producing heat. Since "the word of God is living and active and sharper than any two-edged sword" (Heb.4:12) we can expect discomfort when His Word stays in us.

But fortunately we have the benefit of His Spirit's fruit showing up in our lives. In the Bible, bearing fruit is always a result of intimate relationship with Jesus. It is like osmosis, moving imperceptibly from one person to another. Being in close proximity with Jesus, we catch His attributes as we would catch a cold.

"The fruit of the Spirit is love, joy, peace, patience, kindness, goodness, faithfulness, gentleness, [and] self control" (Gal. 5:22-23). This fruit never will be mine unless I die, stepping aside, and let Jesus take my place. It is fruit of the Spirit, not fruits of the world. I can't go to the market and purchase the Spirit's fruit in the produce department. Nor can I earn them by being good. They are God's free gift to those who abide with Him. They come as "parts included" when I actively invite Jesus into my heart. However, Jesus warned that getting these characteristics usually requires heat. Dying to self is hard—even dangerous. The seed's life reminded me of this.

I have continued to ponder the time the seed spends under ground in utter obscurity. This time of darkness parallels those lonely and depressing times when it seems God has abandoned us. Darkness may represent the drudgery of performing monotonous, unseen, unappreciated tasks. Perhaps it's a portrayal of economic difficulty, a lost job, or fallout from a past relationship. Death and illness can feel like darkness overcoming us.

However, after those times of darkness end, if we are faithful (believing and obeying), God causes us to bloom. Isaiah 49:2 says God puts us into the shadow of His hand until we learn to hear Him. I see how He covered me with His shadow while waiting for me to trust Him. The trees' shadows provide respite from the blistering summer sun, and though they can block sunshine needed for plant growth, shadows also depict the restorative value of darkness.

Parable of the Seeds

Jesus used seeds to illustrate how the seeds of His Word grow exponentially because of the unseen force within them. In Matthew 13:3-9, He says God's Word is like a seed and our hearts are like the soil—rich, rocky, or shallow. Using a farmer sowing seeds in varying soil conditions, He describes our "soul fields." I am fascinated that Jesus chose common, ordinary dirt as the parallel for our hearts.

Some seeds fell along the roadside and were quickly eaten by birds. I picture a thief discovering a house containing many valuables, unoccupied, unguarded, and unlocked. If we don't protect God's Word like a treasure, it easily can be stolen from us. When I first believed in God, I didn't comprehend the enormity of His forgiveness and love. I didn't know the power of His Word, and birds snatched away my seeds. Anything that snatches God's truth away before it has time to take root can be like the birds—people, circumstances, thoughts, anything. Sadly, when I first was a Christian, I valued people's opinions more than God's.

Jesus mentioned other seeds that fell on rocky places. These seeds sprouted quickly, but because there was inadequate depth to the soil, the sun promptly scorched them. Their lack of roots kept their anchor unsecured. Through this picture, Jesus depicts one who meets persecution and quickly abandons the truth.

This, too, applies to my journey. Initially, my soil was but a thin layer, unable to sustain healthy roots. I tended my seeds poorly, shunning them when confronted with doubt or when acceptance was at risk. Even today, if I don't plant God's Word in my heart, reverently pondering its meaning, it can't take root and grow.

Still other seeds fell among thorns that choked them. Does our busyness not squeeze our time with God? Are the beeps, rings, and tones of our technological conveniences so loud that we are deaf to God's whisper? Do the many activities (thorns) growing in our lives smother the seedlings? During my early years with Him, I was so busy trying to perform well that I neglected my seeds. Later, the thorniness of rejection discouraged the growth of new seedlings in my depleted soil.

I identify with each soil type Jesus described. My soil's condition varies—sometimes within the span of a few hours! However, the soil's quality and depth are up to me, and I now recognize a supernatural balance between the soil and the seed. The seeds of God's truth need good, honest hearts to spur growth, and the soil of my heart needs God's Word for its enrichment.

Only by faith can I trust the Holy Spirit to teach me the truths that lie within the seeds. Because "the wisdom of this world is foolishness before God" (1 Cor. 3:19), I need the Holy Spirit to tap into God's wisdom. The Bible says if we lack discernment, we can pray to God and He will send the Holy Spirit to impart wisdom to us (James 1:5).

Occasionally, I receive seeds that simply won't germinate. But the seed Jesus spoke about in His parable is never at fault. If the growth becomes stunted, or never happens at all, the soil is to blame—the recipient of the seed. It is never a problem with the seed. I sometimes blame others for planting hurtful seeds rather than amending my soil with truth.

Since the type of soil affects germination, Jesus challenges us to be careful how we hear the faultless Word of God. Too often, our hearts are hard and crusty. Our spiritual attitudes need adjustments. In Mark 4:23, He says, "If anyone has ears to hear, let him hear."

I can be so devoted to people, decisions, and convictions that I become deaf to God. Hot political issues and cultural shifts can loosen me from God, my anchor, and cause me to refocus, if not obsess, on my (fallible) judgment of correctness. In that kind of legalistic soil, I am likely to lose sight of God's grace, which is the medium in which He chooses to grow me. Just as I keep in touch with a friend to discern her heart, I must stay connected to my heavenly Father and under the umbrella of His grace.

Regrettably, early on I left the seeds of God's Word to life's circumstances. Like fallen seeds in the garden, many were blown away by the winds of working, volunteering, carpooling, or competition. Others were trampled by passing peers and social whims.

We Reap What We Sow

Seeds reproduce their own kind. A sunflower seed cannot produce a zinnia nor does a rudbeckia seed produce a lily. Galatians 6:7 warns us about being deceived, saying that whatever a man sows, he will reap.

Everything we see, hear, smell, taste, and touch is like a tiny seed planted in our minds. If we allow seeds of pride, immorality, jealousy, resentment, greed, or bitterness to be planted, it won't be long before they take root in our hearts. Soon we'll reap an unhealthy harvest, yielding restless souls. However, the Bible says sowing seeds of kindness, gentleness, patience, and love will reap flowers of mercy, joy, and inner peace. That is why Jesus warned, "Take care what you listen to" (Mark 4:24).

I surely reaped a damaged harvest by listening to the wrong voice. I allowed faulty thinking to invade my mind and become a stronghold by not staying connected to Jesus, whose truth heals and frees.

Growing …

Hosea 10:12 tells us to "Sow with a view to righteousness, Reap in accordance with kindness; Break up your fallow ground, For it is time to seek the Lord until He comes to rain righteousness on you." A call to action, this passage commands the sower to sow with a certain outcome in mind: righteousness.

Further action is commanded when the farmer must "break up" his fallow ground, again suggesting effort to prepare the way for the harvest. We Christians too often passively sit back waiting for God to change us, rather than taking responsibility for our actions. However, if we leave our inner ground fallow and untended, we leave its success to chance.

A crop of some variety will grow, be it good or bad, whether or not I offer support. However, it may grow crooked or in an undesirable place, or never attain its full potential. Surely we are to wait on God's guiding to discern our paths, but Jesus was a man of action, always commanding His followers. When Jesus takes us to the edge of a cliff, He asks us to trust Him either to catch us or to teach us to fly. He never tells us to sit on the edge of the cliff! He never will lead me where His grace will not protect me.

In my commercial garden, many of the weeds grew from seeds brought as unwanted gifts from other critters. I once found sunflower seeds in the thick tail fur of my golden retriever, Frances.

While sitting close to me as I planted, she had swept up seeds from the soil with her wagging tail. I anticipated, and subsequently found, sunflowers sprouting in unwanted places around the farm. Likewise, as a child I unknowingly picked up seeds of self-doubt and shame, which took root and sprouted into weeds. The sprouts crowded the good seedlings and spotted the landscape of my soul.

… and Knowing

Each year, in early spring before planting, I submit a soil sample for analysis. This determines which nutrients already flourish in my garden and which ones it lacks. Referring to my flower manual, I decide what type of soil nourishment each flower requires for maximum productivity, and then I make the necessary amendments.

Luke 6:45 tells us, "The good man out of the good treasure of his heart brings forth what is good." Whenever I plant seeds in my garden, I ask myself what seeds I have planted in my life. What can I bring forth from my heart? What is my harvest going to look like? What is the condition of my spiritual soil? Does it need amending? Am I allowing my entertainment, friends, or circumstances to plant seeds of doubt, envy, or failure?

Arrogance, pride, or disillusionment blossom from poor seeding. If good seeds haven't been planted in me, I can't bring forth any lasting good. What a shame we can't send off a soul sample, get an expert analysis, and simply sprinkle the recommended amendments on our lives.

We are exhorted in James 5:7, "Be patient, then, brothers, until the Lord's coming. See how the farmer waits for the land to yield its valuable crop and how patient he is for the autumn and spring rains" (NIV). Waiting for my garden seeds to sprout taught me about faith. When I plant each seed, I believe it will bloom into a flower.

Faith believes without seeing. I cannot see the planted seed, yet I believe the flower will emerge.

Dying to Live

> That which you sow does not come to life unless it dies.
>
> —1 Cor. 15:36

Paul says he dies daily, and later he adds, "For to me, to live is Christ and to die is gain" (Phil. 1:21). Only by dying to self can we live the life Jesus encourages us to live. Just as the seed must die (fall off the flower) and embed in the ground before it can flower, so must we. "Unless a grain of wheat falls into the earth and dies, it remains alone; but if it dies, it bears much fruit" (John 12:24).

Unless we die to our own identity, we can't grow into God's. If we grip onto our worldly image in this life, we won't be able to let go and grasp Jesus' offered life. We produce spiritually only after we let go temporally. Giving up my own selfish desires and adopting my Father's comes in baby steps. It is a process.

It took years before I understood that the blessings of dying to self would far surpass what I tried so hard to achieve on my own. I was a striving kind of Christian, and I needed to yield to the old striver's death. Romans 6:3, which speaks of my baptism as a believer into Jesus' death, came to life as I watched the process of a seed. Its fall and burial in the ground was necessary before it could begin to live as a flower. In a sense, it was baptized in the soil's darkness.

Promises, Promises

In order for the God-seeds to take root and bear fruit, we must believe the promises entrenched deeply in His Word. Obeying His commands guarantees specific results—abundant life and salvation. When I grow my garden, I must scrutinize the grower's manual.

Similarly, I must study God's Word, scrutinizing the steps for growth and His promised outcomes to receive them. I never would have known what to do without regular and repeated reference to my grower's manual.

How many times has your child reminded you of a promise made earlier in an attempt to bring it to fruition? When we are reminded, we feel responsible to be accountable and trustworthy. If we keep our promises, how much more will God keep His? "I will praise you ... because you are faithful to your promises, O my God" (Ps. 71:22 NLT). We, therefore, need to know God's promises so we can remind Him. If the seed could talk, it might remind me of its adoption and my promise to guide, guard, and protect it throughout its life.

Chapter 9

WEEDS: ALL THAT GROWS ISN'T GRAND!

[There is] a time to uproot what is planted.

—Eccl. 3:2

I NEVER HAVE witnessed an invasion where I literally felt overrun and out-maneuvered—until I discovered weeds in my garden. A formidable opponent, weeds persist, gain strength, and grow fast. I once read in a gardening book that anything growing where it was not intended is a weed. I have adopted that definition for my flower garden.

Thousands of weeds chose my two acres as their permanent residence. They can be exhausting to deal with, both mentally and physically. I often traipsed happily to the garden in the cool, early morning, singing as I went. But when I ended up spending priceless hours weeding instead of cutting flowers, both my melody and my vigor fell flat!

Since these weeds took a keen liking to my garden, they built firm foundations with deep roots. These permanent tenants intended to stay. I couldn't evict them for not paying rent. Nor could they simply be cut, like grass, to look nicer on the surface.

The whole plant had to be dug out, including the root, or they would return in a week. Some were so established, I didn't have the physical strength to uproot them. They required a shovel and a big dig, but they had to be extracted for the flowers' well-being.

In early spring, it takes time and scrutiny to decipher the newly emerging weedlings from my precious, rising seedlings. The weeds' initial foliage often looks almost identical to early flower growth. Once I actually transplanted fifty or more weedlings to my garden, convinced they were a favorite wildflower I wanted to establish. It took the better part of a day to plant these imposters, and required much bending, kneeling, and digging—sweat equity, which was greatly needed in the kitchen, laundry room, yard, and barn.

By the time the weeds grew tall enough to be identified as such, my chosen baby seedlings were competing for survival. With frustration, I wondered how I could be so easily duped.

God Waters the Garden, but He Doesn't Weed It

Weeds so wonderfully represent one way the enemy works to stumble us. Jesus says in John 10:10, "The thief comes only to steal and kill and destroy; I came that they may have life, and have it abundantly." The weed thieves from my garden. It robs the seedlings of water and nutrients available underground. The flowers get crowded. They, like me, need space to wiggle their toes and feel the sunshine on their faces. Weeds also steal my joy by engaging me in a battle I did not intend to fight. They substitute my promised abundant life with mediocrity.

If I am not careful, I become a slave to the weeds, and they become my master. They dictate my goals. I must continually focus on why I fight the war on weeds—it's for the flowers. The flowers are worth the battle, so I must not obsess over the weeds, but cling to my initial love intention.

In life, I can be so consumed with good activities that I miss the opportunity to harvest the day's "flowers"—too busy tending the roses to stop and smell them. If I volunteer for a worthy cause but neglect my family, then perhaps volunteering should be transplanted. At times I committed myself or my children to so many worthwhile pursuits that we lacked quality time together—there was no time to relax. Even church work can diminish time alone with God. Easily distracted, I sometimes give more of me to good works than to God Himself. However, He didn't ask me to work *for* Him, but rather to allow Him to work in me.

Weedy and Needy

One day I noticed a perfect cleome in my zinnia bed. Although the cleome bloomed magnificently in its designated row, I did not want a cleome invading my zinnias. Therefore, the cleome was a weed in that row. If I had allowed the cleome to stay, it would have shed its seeds among the zinnias, creating a mixed bed.

Because mine was a market garden, I needed to keep the two flowers separate. They require unique treatments and have different growth patterns. In a typical country garden, the two flowers would mix beautifully, but a market garden is planted for efficiency and production. I stopped, took a load off my clogs, and pondered the parable under the shade of a nearby tree.

Many things in life look good and indeed are good, but if they are out of place they become detrimental. However, the very thought of killing the cleome appeared more a tragedy than a responsibility. Since it was a spectacular thirty inches tall, a perfect specimen, I decided to use it in an arrangement. After carefully digging up the remaining stem and root ball, I transplanted it back where it belonged with the rest of the cleome clan. The cleome, in and of itself, was a prize, but it had become a weed when in the wrong place.

As I journaled the week's events, I saw weeds in my life as well. What robs my joy, peace, and contentment, and prevents me from achieving my goals? What requires too much of my time and energy—be it physical, emotional, or mental? I found many "good" things that needed to be set aside. And as I apprehensively let them go, God's love filled the spaces, and faith in Him sustained me.

Root of Pride

Weeds come in many shapes and sizes. Even some people we admire can become weeds, demanding time and energy and competing for our water, nutrients, and the Son. They may need to be moved to another row.

When identifying something or someone as a weed, I sometimes hesitate to move it. But now is not the time to falter. I must pull it up by its roots and transplant it. Yet Pride whispers, "Who will know it is a weed? Let it stay." Volunteering to bake a cake for the sick appears unselfish but actually can cover a self-seeking motivation. How much of my benevolence is done to make me feel good about myself?

My adversary knows my weaknesses and my sinful nature all too well. He frequently appeals to his cohort, Pride, who craftily suggests I avoid anyone or anything that might damage my worldly appearance. Satan always makes me think about me, not God. Hiding his oft-mistaken identity, Pride deters me from asking for forgiveness. To do so, he implies subtly, would be admitting my fault, weakening my foundation.

He stunts my growth. Yet I am slow to recognize my sly motivation because of its very nature. One of Pride's many subtleties caused me to hold myself to a higher standard than I held for others. Continuing to raise the bar, I created unattainable expectations. Though weary of the pursuit, I was scared to admit failure, bury the old striver, and attend the funeral.

Even confession can become a thing of pride. If I am unguarded, my brokenness may become a satisfaction and my humility twisted into conceit. Sadness, abuse, or tragedy can become badges we wear, like martyrs. Convincing us that we deserve sympathy, attention, or even praise for suffering, Pride assures us we have earned the honor. However, only in humble godly submission does our brokenness provide access to the throne of grace. Last week I heard a friend defending her sorrow, claiming it to be greater than another's. How deceiving the enemy is. Steadfast honesty before God is imperative for a weed-free soul.

Wheat or Tare?

I recently witnessed the wheat harvesting at Cowlick Farm. Tares, or weeds, that resembled wheat grew amid the stalks. During the height of growing season, it was difficult to distinguish between the two. However, at harvest time, the heads, or seedpods, of the wheat bowed down, whereas the tares stood up straight. To represent the wheat Jesus spoke of in the parable of the tares (see Matt. 13:36-40), we must humbly bow before Him and submit our pride to His will. Those who are not "hearers of the Word," the tares, refuse to bow to the Great Harvester.

Satan always finds something pretty, interesting, intellectual, charming, or self-gratifying to sidetrack me. If the distraction were earmarked "weed," I'd simply remove it, but I am easily fooled.

I saw this manifested clearly in my garden. Knowing weeds can look nearly identical to flowers, I take the time to carefully inspect any new, emerging sprout I find. I first scrutinize the leaf, comparing it to the leaf of the flower I intend to grow. A tiny notch on the tip may be the only difference. Perhaps the leaves' soft or rough feel classifies the flower's identity. By going back to the plant I am sure of, I can decide if the one in question is an imposter. We know people by their "fruits" or attributes (see Matt. 7:16). In life, by referring to Jesus as the One of whom I can be sure, I can discern truth from its pretender.

On Guard: Deception Not Allowed

I am quicker now to identify noxious weeds in my soul's garden. In the past, pride kept me from listening to the still, small voice. Even saying, "God called me to write this book" has drawn cynical comments and questions. Discouraged, I'm tempted to say nothing, or not to write the book at all, to avoid criticism.

Peer pressure at any age is a weed in my soul garden. Spontaneously placing the opinion of others above my heavenly Father's endorsement, I sometimes withhold comments about my Christian perspective. As I confessed earlier, I struggled to stand alone on principle and not seek approval. I still ask myself, "Did I stay quiet out of godly discernment or to avoid ridicule?" Only by studying God's Word am I able to distinguish between the results of pride and the results of seeking God. Just as I remove imposters in the flower garden, I ask God to weed out that ol' cheat, Pride, from my soul garden.

Good Weeds?

Though demoralizing, weeds compose a natural part of any garden. Part of God's creation, weeds serve useful purposes. They can appear lovely growing beside the road or in a distant field. They also provide food and shelter for critters. Many quail at Cowlick Farm survive by finding refuge among the weeds and tall grasses. Weeds can also minimize erosion.

Just as healthy rivalry can command us to better performance, competition also profits the natural arena. We have planted many pine seedlings at Cowlick farm. It takes several years for them to grow tall enough to be recognized as pine trees. During their early adolescence, many taller wild seedlings surround them. Temporarily, they are almost indistinguishable in their little forest.

It's not until years later that the baby pines actually soar above the rest. In this case, the weeds help by forcing the young trees to grow straight and tall in their instinctive upward reach for sun.

In the garden, however, that competition for survival often diminishes the flower's livelihood. In life, what works for one may be another's downfall. Without divine guidance, how can we ever really know? Jesus called me to live in the world, but not to be *of* it and not to be consumed by it. Life thrusts us into the rushed pace of urban life, but Jesus, while acknowledging that, calls us to rest our souls in an unseen garden with Him. He uses my particular trials to mold me into the shape He wants, and may use similar hardships in a different way with others. I now see the heartache that drove me to God as a gift rather than a loss.

God gives us free will to choose how we live, view situations, and handle tough times. He doesn't interfere in every decision, vetoing our bad choices. However, He does promise to use our difficulties to progress our journey, if we ask. My weeds can be the very circumstances He uses to strengthen my character. How I handle them is the important thing. His discipline does not punish, but instructs. Just as the pine tree naturally strives to soar above the wild saplings, God instills in me the desire to reach past my hurts to new heights in Him.

Ditch-bank Blessings

I once had contracted to create flower arrangements for a special affair. The client chose tulips because they would be in peak form at the time. Approaching the garden the day prior to the engagement, I found them all gone, cut down to within inches of the ground. Bambi had apparently entertained his friends the night before and served my tulips as the main entrée.

I was devastated, if not panicked. It was early in the season, and my other flowers were not yet blooming in abundance. "What will I do? How can I fulfill my obligation?" I took a walk in the woods with Frances, my golden retriever, and Pete, my English setter. I confessed to the Lord my neediness and frustration, and my temptation to quit this business yet again.

My soliloquy barely finished, I looked up and saw the ditch bank covered with pink. "Flowers? Weeds? Where did they come from?" I queried aloud. "I've never seen these, and I've walked this path hundreds of times. Do I dare use these as the mainstays for my contract?"

No verbal response came from my four-legged companions, but they sensed my excitement and, tails wagging, spontaneously shared the joy. I hurried back to the barn, collected my clippers, gloves, and a basket, and returned to the scene of the miracle. Hundreds, if not thousands, of dainty pink flowers fluttered on multiple ditch banks. Wonder washed over me as I rejoiced in my Lord's hand at work again. His almighty provision humbly reminded me of His grace despite my own faltering faith.

I hadn't noticed the wildflowers, though they were present all along. They recalled my imaginary but real playmates. God had given me all I needed. It is I who did not see and partake, not He who withheld. How blind I am, often missing the blessings shining in plain view. When my plans go awry, I sometimes think I am left to manage alone, as I felt in the upstairs bedroom when I cried out to God from the depth of loneliness. But my first response should be to ask God to show me the way and to believe He will.

How many other flowers am I missing? He used those simple weeds to teach me a valuable lesson. The whole ordeal, I now see, wasn't about the flowers or the contract at all. God entered my world, met me there, and taught me.

Chapter 10

COMPOSTING: GIVE IT UP

The old things passed away; behold, new things have come.
—2 Cor. 5:17

DETERMINED TO MAKE the honor roll in Gardening 101, I spent untold hours poring over garden books in a worn-out, springs-sprung Barnes & Noble chair. Sipping on a white mocha, I investigated the subject of composting. Consistently I discovered this advice for constructing a compost bin:

1. Locate it out of sight—it is not pretty.
2. Position it away from the house—it can smell bad.
3. Locate it near enough to be convenient.

Additionally, the ingredients need air, rain, and sun, but mostly time. I diligently followed the recommendations. My compost pile was well away from my house and in a good position to receive the air, rain, and sun it needed.

Webster's defines compost as "a fertilizer mixture, especially one containing decayed leaves and manure, lime, etc., mixed in a pile."[3] Anything that came from the ground originally will disintegrate and can be used to make compost. *Aha!* All that lettuce, cabbage, and collards Peter Rabbit and his friends nibbled in my garden for hors d'oeuvres last night are not totally wasted. The scraps they left in the veggie patch could be of great value.

Several days later, I eagerly gathered their leftovers and began the new pile. In addition, I scooped up horse manure and added it to the collection. Grass clippings, leaves, dead flowers, hay, pine straw, and ashes from the fireplace heaped it even higher. I was well on the way to earning an "A" in this self-taught class.

Inside I kept a bowl near the kitchen sink for compost material. I added coffee grounds, eggshells, broccoli stems, and carrot and potato peelings, for starters. The collection always drew negative comments from friends. It was not a pretty sight. Since composting felt like a school project, and I was aiming to be valedictorian, the accumulation continued. Every few days, when my kitchen bowl filled or the contents became decayed enough to disgust even me, I dumped it on the enlarging mound.

I was to layer the vegetable matter between the manure and soil. Nitrogen in the manure made the pile more biologically active. The compost heated up because of this microbial activity. Microorganisms and earthworms digested the particles and converted it into enriched compost, which nourishes the plants. The more worms, the better. (This pile later became a gold mine for the fishermen in my life.)

The process takes from a few weeks up to a year, depending on the size and content of the refuse material and variables in the environment. Regardless of how colorful my culinary endeavors had been (orange carrot peels, red onions, yellow squash, or green broccoli) the final product always turned dark brown. Typically, the kitchen collection still could be identified for many days. However, after stirring and sufficient time, even their individual identity melded into the others. They became part of the whole new substance.

Holy Heat

Dead to sin, but alive to God in Christ Jesus.

—Rom. 6:11

One day while mixing this rotting mass with the backhoe, I was shocked to see smoke escaping from deep within. I felt the heat from eight feet away. I stared in awe. The Lord spoke as clearly (though not audibly) as if my husband had asked what was for dinner. From the specifics of locating the pile, to the disintegration of the discarded scraps, the progression became another parable for God's Word.

Everything in the heap was dead or dying. As it became a refashioned substance with a different purpose, it was born again, becoming a new entity.

A favorite song came to mind and the words played softly on my lips:

> Give them all, give them all, give them all to Jesus
> Shattered dreams, wounded hearts, broken toys
> Give them all, give them all, give them all to Jesus
> And He will turn your sorrows into joy.

Humbled by God's touch, I longed to gather my hurts, and those of my loved ones, and throw them onto that smoldering pile. Changes were taking place deep inside me, making me crave restoration and a new identity, too. I wanted to be "born again"—again.

I sat, asked, and wondered. What is this deep, nagging ache in my spirit? Where does this void come from? What wound is lodged in my heart? I longed for my brokenness to be transformed into wholeness.

Allowing God to show me my true, sinful nature is not a night at the theater. I don't always agree with God's assessment immediately, and I sometimes argue. *Me, prideful? Unforgiving? Nonsense!* I prefer to revel in my best self and my accomplishments. But my outward actions reveal the heat inside me. The slow-burning embers of anger, fear, resentment, and regret remain hidden at first, but if you stir me up, their presence seeps out.

My insecurity causes me to defend my sin, disguise it, or argue that it has value. For instance, I may say the reason I did not confront a friend was to spare her hurt, when actually I was avoiding my own fear of exposure or rejection. Or I may excuse my unrighteous anger, claiming it was the impetus that got me over a hurdle. And rather than sincerely requesting prayer for a friend's misfortune, I may use it as an opportunity to make my own behavior appear superior.

Not Now, Lord—Maybe Later

I don't always feel ready when God chooses to expose my sin. His timing often seems inconvenient to my agenda: "Surely You don't want me to address this issue right before Christmas, do You, Lord? It will ruin the holidays for my family." Sin stubbornly fights to retain its old colors. It also likes its well-worn easy chair at my soul's fireside.

Yet when I honestly ask God for the truth, I hear His quiet voice, feel His subtle nudge, and recognize my wrongdoing. Eventually, I confess and ask for forgiveness, seeking salvage for my scraps. He brings no condemnation. However, before I fully compute the vast implication that I am forgiven, an inner conflict ensues.

Confession, like the nitrogen, speeds my old nature's decomposition. Smoke leaks, and the prideful me wants to hang on to those tangible things that bring worldly fulfillment. My emotional temperature rises. That old, selfish me wars against the newly birthed creature in me. There is not enough room for both of them. One has to go, but both walk my soul's pathways. In the search for God's truth, I witness this clash almost daily. I still struggle with letting go of the labels I wore as a child.

Turn Up the Heat

In our everyday lives, high temperatures cleanse and disinfect. Dirty dishes, laundry, and medical instruments all benefit from heat. In the Bible, fire symbolizes purification. To remove impurities, a silversmith leaves his metal in the fire until his image reflects back. God allows us to stay in the fire until He can see Himself in us. He knows the refinement that results from the heat.

A potter employs his kiln's heat to set his craft. Likewise, God uses life's heat to set His creations. He said to Jeremiah, "Behold, like the clay in the potter's hand, so are you in My hand" (Jer. 18:6). God delights in re-crafting us on His wheel. I am still spinning.

Situations in life expose my heart's contents. Sometimes the heat is unbearable. I'd rather walk a mile in high heels than feel so miserable in my own skin! Just as the coffee grounds transformed into fresh compost, by submitting my past to Jesus I also have a fresh start. Our old sinful selves are composted into something new when Jesus lives in us. "I have been crucified with Christ; and it is no longer I who live, but Christ lives in me" (Gal. 2:20).

Location, Location, Location

A vital part of the metaphor—locating the unattractive and often smelly pile out of sight—added to my understanding. Acknowledging my rotting private actions, attitudes, or motivations can be demoralizing. Dumped together, they are not a pretty sight either. They stink!

When Jesus told the disciples to remove the stone from Lazarus's tomb, Martha warned of bad odors. He had been dead several days (see John 11:39). Are we not fearful, like Martha, that our hidden sins will smell when exposed? Are we not more comfortable with a stone hiding our tomb than a light shining in?

I buried shameful things in my soul's grave. Though they were decaying and needed to be let out, I nevertheless guarded that secret place like an armed night watchman. God sent Jesus so I would not have a tomb to guard. The despair trapped inside me was never meant to stay there. Whatever is hidden in fear ends up spoiling, turning my heart sour.

Share the Proceeds

Just as the compost pile needs to be positioned apart, I prefer to be away from human traffic, alone with the Composter, when the decomposition begins. My attention needs to be focused on Him, not surrounding distractions. But the resulting product, renewed and healthy, needs to be spread, even if words never are used. As a disciple, I am called to share the transformed compostings with others as a witness of my Father. Because of His renewing work, my life reflects regeneration.

Peel It Off, Scoop It Out

For you have died and your life is hidden with Christ in God.
—Col. 3:3

The peelings, scoopings, and shells on the compost pile provide another powerful image. They represent hang-ups, disappointments, regrets, and sins. Holding on to them adds to my load. Their weight encumbers me from living the abundant life. Carrying a heavy load disrupts my rest, and rest is required to complete the journey. Excess baggage also complicates the trip for my traveling companions. Each item in the pile symbolized a burden I needed to get rid of:

- Fireplace ashes/fear and insecurity: Fear of being hurt kept me from enjoying relationships and life. The antithesis of trusting God, fear holds its owner hostage. I distanced myself, if only emotionally, when I feared the rejection that could come if I was exposed at my core.
- Eggshells/unforgiveness: Holding a grudge only adds extra weight. I don't have the power to forgive a past hurt anyway. Only in releasing it to God can I be set free. Vengeance is God's, not my, responsibility.
- Peelings/anxiety: Financial, social, or health anxieties portray a lack of faith in my heavenly Father who promises to be my sufficiency. Worry also diminishes present satisfaction.
- Coffee grounds/bitterness: The heartache that remains from the long-ago actions of a loved one can become bitter and continue to sour my perspective.
- Onion skins/jealousy: Struggling with resentment toward friends whose pampered lives made mine seem unfair, I became judgmental, critical, and self-righteous. Pride keeps me from admitting my envy.
- Decaying stalks/self pity: The quiet self-pity I nursed when others received recognition while I was ignored also needed to be rooted out. My dad's death filled my inner chambers with gloom, and feeling unloved by my husband caused sadness, angst, and despair—all trappings that needed to go.

If any of the scraps linger in the bowl or if the manure stays in the stall, they remain scraps and manure, smelly and useless. However, by putting them on the compost pile, the bowl and the stall are cleaned, and the discards find new life.

The After Effect

Come to Me, all who are weary and heavy-laden, and I will give
you rest.

—Matt. 11:28

A heap of compost adds nourishment to the flowers in my
garden, and the flowers, in turn, bring beauty to any room and cheer
to weary souls. But to get these marvelous results, the ingredients
first must be submitted to the pile. The compost cannot enrich
until it endures the long decaying process. The chance of producing
compost without surrendering items to be composted is zero.

What are your coffee grounds and tough stalks? What are your
broken eggshells? Do you suffer humiliation or regrets from your
past? I sure did. Are you postponing self-examination to delay
painful realities, too? If you see the hard truth, are you willing to
take the required action and pay a personal cost?

Years ago I feared the cost of disruption to my busy life would
be too high. After all, I'd dreamed of being a wife and mom since
childhood. I couldn't let it crumble. I feared the detour exposing
every facet of my hurt would take.

Despite my trepidation, with God's help I methodically gave
over these areas of my life, tossing them onto the pile. I now seek
a composted life in Jesus, just as I thirst for water in the sweltering
heat of a backbreaking workday in my garden.

Trusting the Transformer

When God rebuked His people for their disobedience, He called
them to repentance, telling them, "Though your sins are as scarlet,
they will be as white as snow; though they are red like crimson,
they will be like wool" (Isa. 1:18). Nothing is too big, bad, or ugly
for our Lord to compost if we trust Him. Our corrupt humanness
makes a God who really will forgive and forget all our scoopings

unfathomable! But He promised. Oh, the years I wasted hiding my regrets and bearing them alone. The psalmist writes, "As far as the east is from the west, so far has He removed our transgressions from us" (Ps. 103:12).

I was "weary and heavy-laden" and desired that heart-rest Jesus promised to those who submit their burdens to Him. I wanted to feel the relaxed pace of His grace. I eventually realized I could not purify myself, compensate for sin, or erase the past anymore than the egg could mend its crack or the horse refine its manure. Waiting on nature gives them new life. Wiping my slate clean is the sovereign work of an almighty God. The Holy Spirit identified what needed to be discarded, and I trusted the Transformer to do His job.

Resurrection

Taste and see that the Lord is good.

—Ps. 34:8

I saw the Easter message in that smoldering pile—Jesus' torture, crucifixion, death, burial, and resurrection. The composted elements were tortured as I scraped, chopped, and discarded them as worthless. They died and were buried in the pile. And they were resurrected, though it took longer than three days. According to *Webster's,* resurrection is an act of rising from an inferior state into a superior one; a transference from death to life. It is a restoration and a revival. My meager scoopings and scrapings definitely transformed from an inferior state to a superior existence as nourishing fertilizer.

In Philippians 3:7-8 (KJV), Paul said, "But what things were gain to me, those I counted loss for Christ. Yea doubtless, and I count all things but loss for the excellency of the knowledge of Christ Jesus my Lord: for whom I have suffered the loss of all things, and do count them but dung, that I may win Christ." The word *dung* shows how utterly insignificant the apostle Paul esteemed everything except Jesus' gospel.

Paul, a highly regarded man, freely gave up his best worldly things, considering them as dung compared to Christ's riches. He became grateful for his earthly losses because that opened his heart to knowing Jesus intimately. His priorities reversed and his value system inverted. As he weakened his grasp on the world, Paul realized a profound and exhilarating freedom. When we transact with God, He transforms, redeems, and wastes nothing. Absorbing Paul's statement, I again identified with him as I became almost eager to relinquish my worldliness and grasp God.

Take a Look

> Be anxious for nothing, but in everything by prayer and supplication with thanksgiving let your requests be made known to God.
>
> —Phil. 4:6

God knows about our broken shells, and He prepared a place for us to compost them:

> In Me you may have peace. In the world you have tribulation, but take courage; I have overcome the world.
>
> —John 16:33

We spend much time, money, and energy trying to cover them up, but Jesus said to be anxious for nothing, to give them all to Him. Acts 14:22 tells us we must go through many hardships before entering God's kingdom. For years I carried my insecurities like items in a purse, not knowing I could dispose of them.

Jesus encouraged, "My grace is sufficient for you, for power is perfected in weakness" (2 Cor. 12:9). Then Paul continues the paradox, "For when I am weak, then I am strong" (2 Cor. 12:10). God gave Paul a "thorn" in his flesh that restrained his pride. The (undisclosed) thorn produced humility that kept him seeking Jesus, who was his strength.

Even Jesus suffered to the point of death on the cross before He was resurrected. However, it was in that moment of ultimate physical weakness that He became our strength, fulfilled His appointed destiny, and achieved His divine purpose. Is it not in our darkest times that we turn to God for help? The instant I see my weakness, acknowledge my need, and seek God, He immediately steps in.

Having all I want actually obstructs my vision of Jesus. I had to become so uncomfortable with my life that I finally turned completely to God, emptying my purse before Him. As He shined the spotlight on my needy heart's contents, I humbly accepted His love in their place. Contentment replaced emptiness, and my heart began to rest.

De-masking

In 1 Peter 5:6-7 we are exhorted, "Humble yourselves under the mighty hand of God, that He may exalt you at the proper time, casting all your anxiety on Him, because He cares for you." Humility comes before being exalted. It is a prerequisite. As long as we proudly think ourselves sufficient, God can do nothing for us. Oswald Chambers said sin is deliberate and determined independence from God.

Vulnerability comes when we remove our façade, unmasking what hides underneath. But Jesus calls us to do just that:

> After you have suffered for a little while, the God of all grace, who called you to His eternal glory in Christ, will Himself perfect, confirm, strengthen and establish you.
>
> —1 Peter 5:10

If we confess our sins, He is faithful and righteous to forgive us our sins and to cleanse us from all unrighteousness.

—1 John 1:9

When I first confessed, allowing God's light to flood my dungeon cell, I wanted only to hide. It was not a warm fuzzy time with God, but rather a specific, radical event. Nonetheless, that first ray of light strengthened, confirmed, and established me in a new way. I gained new vision as I underwent spiritual composting.

No Pain, No Gain

I have been crucified with Christ.

—Gal. 2:20

Composting takes action on my part. I have to take the initiative to peel the carrot (separate the good from the bad), collect the peelings (acknowledge they are no longer good for me), and put them on the pile (give them up).

I cannot go back and retrieve them. They must remain for nature to have her way. This process helped me see that God won't take that first step for me. He provided a way, but He won't force me. I must surrender my sin, like walking away from the pile and leaving my personal scraps behind. That's my part.

I cannot make the compost. Jesus does that:

If anyone is in Christ, he is a new creature; the old things passed away; behold, new things have come.

—2 Cor. 5:17

God was there for me all those years ago when I refused to expose my layers of deceit and discard my secrets. On the cross, Jesus took my scraps and provided a life of grace.

John 3:30 says, "He must increase, but I must decrease." The discarded refuse decreases as individual entities, yet the pile grows! As I leave my sin at the foot of the cross, I lighten my load, but my faith grows. Peeling off my old sin nature like an onionskin develops the person at my core. After all, I was created in God's image. Years of layering (and each layer created another layer to cover the cover-up) pushed down my regrettable past. My old self must decrease daily, allowing room for Jesus to increase.

Pounded and Grounded

> We are afflicted in every way, but not crushed; perplexed, but not despairing; persecuted, but not forsaken; struck down, but not destroyed.
>
> —2 Cor. 4:8-9

Just as flour is sifted before being baked into bread, eggs are broken before being mixed into cake batter. Each required a "painful" process and endured great heat before reaching its destiny. We see the process all around us every day—coffee beans are ground, nails are pounded, metal is heated and welded. Why do we struggle so with the concept of our own pain and suffering?

Our society doesn't reward brokenness. Instead, it is a weakness to be avoided at great cost. We prefer to ridicule or pity the broken and flaunt our own unbrokenness. The media highlight the strong and successful. Our worldly system applauds those who appear to hold it all together. "No matter the cost, don't be broken!"

Yet we are a culture of broken marriages, homes, and promises. Our worldly stability has cracks at every level and nothing is absolutely secure, but we avoid confession and fight to remain in control, appearing unbroken. We refuse to identify and compost our fractures. Though willing to sacrifice quality time, rest, conscience, or the family jewels, we hide our weakness.

However, we all know that sorrow eventually penetrates our walls of earthly strength. Even the tiara didn't keep doubt from infiltrating my teenage joy.

Beauty Is

> God sees not as man sees, for man looks at the outward appearance, but the Lord looks at the heart.
>
> —1 Sam. 16:7

Any serious gardener knows the value, even beauty, of a compost pile, but most city folks would be repulsed to see it beside my house. Surely this proves that beauty is in the eye of the beholder! God is the Most Serious Gardener and He sees my value. He looks at me as finished compost, not broken shells and horse manure.

At my age, my vessel's decomposing process shows. This body suit I have been loaned is gradually wearing out. My stalks are decaying! I need eyeglasses most of the time. I struggle to get up after a long sitting spell, I frequently strain to hear, and my body makes noises like an old house! Proverbs 20:29 says the honor of old men is their gray hair. If this applies to women also, I am becoming more honorable daily. My earthly clay pot has numerous hairline fractures and chips, but I know this body is only a temporary residence, and I am thankful to use the space.

"The mind set on the flesh is death, but the mind set on the Spirit is life and peace" (Rom. 8:6). On my farm, I look past the useless refuse in the pile and see valuable compost. In life, when I experience the death of a loved one or strain in a relationship, I first respond with loneliness, hurt, rejection, or anxiety. However, through faith in God's promises, I come to see new beginnings.

What a blessing—to set our minds on the things of the Spirit, not of the world! When we look at what God can do, rather than wallowing in our difficulties, we gain freedom in Christ. A worldly mind finds ludicrous the very thought of gaining by losing, but Jesus said, "Whoever seeks to keep his life will lose it, and whoever loses his life will preserve it" (Luke 17:33). Only in relinquishing, can I find lasting joy.

The words of the song I recalled when I first gazed at the rotting pile summarized the essence of the lesson so sweetly:

> Oh, give Him all your tears and sadness,
> Give Him all your years of pain,
> And you'll enter into life in Jesus' name.

Chapter 11

PRUNING:
OUCH, THAT HURTS

He prunes it so that it may bear more fruit.
—John 15:2

IMAGINE SEEING SOMEONE you love approach with long-handled shears (loppers). With no warning, he or she lops off your arm because it sticks out too far. Then, adding insult to injury, the loved one shows no sympathy for your pain and humiliation. Such is the plant's likely perspective on pruning.

The literal meaning of pruning as defined by *Webster's* is "to trim...to cut off...to remove dead or living parts from (a plant) so as to increase fruit or flower production or improve the form.... to cut out or get rid of, as unnecessary parts..."[4] Every gardener understands the necessity of pruning, and we all know how the pruning shears can make a shrub look naked.

I will never forget, years ago, my shock at seeing the beautiful red tip hedge between my neighbor's house and mine reduced to stubs. I announced to myself, "What a tragedy. The pruner has ruined the hedge!" Due to my horticultural ignorance, I thought the hedge was destroyed. Without all the pretty, green, leafy stems, it offered no more shade, no softness or beauty. It remained bare and unattractive, destitute, for a season or two, but by the next year it had grown back healthier than before. In the second year, it was actually gorgeous.

The same principle applies in my flower garden, though initially I was slow to prune as necessary. For many flowers, such as snapdragons and lisianthus, pinching off the first emerging bud stimulates more growth. However, having waited so long for the little darling to finally emerge, pinching it off just didn't feel right. But I was obedient to the flower experts' advice, and it worked.

The Bible says, "For those whom the Lord loves He disciplines, and He scourges every son whom He receives" (Heb. 12:6). We are told discipline is an act of love: "My son, do not reject the discipline of the Lord, or loathe His reproof, for whom the Lord loves He reproves, even as a father corrects the son in whom he delights" (Prov. 3:11-12). What feels like suffering may actually be the Lord's discipline.

God doesn't send tragedy, but He works it for good in our lives, to teach, grow, and develop our character. As a human parent, I made decisions concerning my children that felt painful to them, but out of love I allowed their discomfort.

Sharpen the Shears

If the flower had feelings, pruning would be painful and humiliating. No flower would seek my companionship, knowing my methods not only hurt, but also cause it to look unattractive. In my spiritual life, it often seems I get the opposite of what I pray for. Who hasn't prayed for patience, only to receive trials requiring waiting? I have been pruned and it hurts. It leaves me feeling vulnerable. Never in the moment of shearing do I rejoice. But through the years I've learned that after the initial pruning, if I recommit myself to God, trusting Him with the outcome, I sprout new growth.

For example, using the garden, God pruned my self-sufficiency, confidence, and pride, teaching me to trust Him. No amount of physical labor could keep the garden weed-free. Perfection is not possible in a garden. My best efforts often produced disappointing results. Certain flowers never reached their advertised height nor mirrored their pictured blooms, and many simply refused to thrive in my garden's soil. I had run into something I could not conquer alone.

It was a humbling picture of my life, which I had tried desperately to keep productive and beautiful. The garden reflected my personal neediness and insufficiency with clarity, and I learned the necessity of staying connected to my Source of strength. In the heat of the day, however, it just felt like despair.

I often have misread my emotions, confusing them with faith, and celebrating the joy as coming from God, but never the pain. I looked at hurting as a flower would look at pruning—simply painful and not a necessity for future growth. While surely a byproduct of knowing God, good feelings are not the essence of faith. I have judged God to be absent because of how I felt. However, as in the example of the red tips, looks can be deceiving. I am more careful now to distinguish between the actual fact of God's presence and the feeling. Now I see that the absence of conflict in my life isn't always proof of God's blessing. Remaining on His wheel means He finds me worthy of His refining work.

When I made the initial commitment to believe in Jesus, I didn't feel any different, so I believed God had failed to change me. Instead of trusting in God's foolproof Word, I trusted my own experience. Now I understand that when God seems the most distant, He is cutting away the chaff, as He did when I melted in His arms in total despair. He loves me enough to prune me. After His pruning shears have clipped my flittering wings, I will bloom again a little nearer to the shape He has in mind for me.

Management Control

Just as a good mother disciplines her child, so God disciplines us. We parents think we know the path our children's lives should take, and we prune their little branches to stimulate growth. A favorite pastime may be forbidden because of disobedience or a privilege withheld to allow study time. When mine were young, I denied them desserts if meat, veggies, or fruit weren't eaten first.

These acts of love by a caring parent are not harsh punishments. An undisciplined, disobedient child is not attractive, and the parent does the child a great disservice to withhold godly discipline. If we parents lovingly long to shape our children, how much more does our heavenly Father want to shape us?

God began pruning me of my need to control even before I knew it was necessary! Spouses and children can be effective loppers in God's hands, for who can live with another without having to relinquish some control? For instance, my husband's concept of a well made bed, a clean house, appropriate attire, or effective communication are as different from mine as Greek is from English. On many occasions, I have re-done or corrected what he attempted, whether it was washing a dish, loading the car, or answering a question merely because it wasn't done my way—the right way!

Now much of our home décor is a response to his habits or practicality, or to accommodate his needs rather than my personal preferences. For marital preservation, I withhold many verbal corrections! I have relinquished control, though I haven't always acquiesced to his choices with enthusiasm. Regrettably, I have often criticized his actions (if only to myself) rather than praising his efforts.

I am still learning to let go when others approach things differently, whether it is my mom, sisters, husband, children, friends, or co-workers. This is difficult because I like the world to sway to my rhythm. God regularly snips at my controlling branches and it still smarts.

Cutting Back

It is recommended that certain plants such as forsythias and azaleas be pruned right after they finish blooming. Imagine losing your radiance, charm, and beauty suddenly. Then, along with your shock over the loss, you are also cut to your core. It would be incredibly painful unless you trusted your gardener to know exactly what he was doing. Knowing you'd be far more striking the next time you bloomed would also help.

We never choose to be hurt. But Jesus calls us to say, "Thank You, God, for loving me enough to prune me into the shape You want." John 15:2 says, "Every branch in Me that does not bear fruit, He takes away; and every branch that bears fruit, He prunes it so that it may bear more fruit." God is not wary of my anger or misunderstanding. He, like a good parent, but with perfect wisdom, will do what is necessary for my growth. Because He wants me to be fruitful, He will use His shears to make me more productive.

Answering the call to write this book has required me to set aside things that previously occupied my time—many that were good. God pruned me of desires and distractions that I might finish what He exhorted me to do: be fruitful for Him. It has not always been pleasurable, nor understood by others, but I knew His shears were at work. It took a serious accident to curtail my activities and create the time and focus to write. I don't believe He caused the injury, but, like a tree broken in a storm that sprouts new growth afterward, I believe He used the ordeal to grow me.

God always keeps His eyes on His goal, which is to bring me into His kingdom for eternal fellowship with Him. Not worried about offending me, He loves with a perfect, tough love. He may even remove those things in which I find security so I can distinguish between Him and the world's pleasures. Using my empty nest, He refocused my priorities. Since mothering had provided a safe haven where I flourished, reorienting, though difficult, sprouted new growth. Suffering, in any form, reveals my need for a deep connection with Jesus and trains me to exercise my faith even when my spirit is forlorn.

God may also need to prune those things about which I am passionate. Frequent self-examination helps. "What activities take up space on my daily planner? Am I more dedicated to working, exercising, planning, or shopping than I am to my heavenly Father? Do I focus more at work, at lunch, watching television, or perusing magazines than on God? What thoughts occupy most of my time?"

It is not that God wants me apathetic about my dreams, loves, or circumstances. It is rather that He wants my deepest yearning to be for Him. He snips at my pettiness and immature commitments regularly to redirect my growth, which actually stimulates my heart's core desires (which come from Him).

As long as I have passions apart from God, He will do whatever He must to turn my heart back to Him. He is always waiting—wooing me into friendship. My dreams come from God and my job is to submit them to Him for His interpretation and completion. He is the Author of passion and He wants to awaken our longings. We wrongly assume God will somehow remove our passions if we confess them. But I find He enhances the depth and intensity of my yearnings when I submit them to Him. He uses what may seem worldly for otherworldly purposes.

In a healthy marriage, each spouse wants the other to pursue his or her individual passions, hobbies, or interests, but we always want to remain the number-one crave and first (earthly) priority of our mate. So it is with God, but the stakes are for eternity.

I am learning to invite Him into my passions. Initially, market gardening consumed my days, allowing no time for worship. By inviting God to garden with me, He opened my eyes to a new reality, causing me to view life through a different lens. Not only did He not remove my passion, He increased my productivity and joy.

Loppers in the Wrong Hands

While writing this book, I experienced another painful pruning. A loved one who scorned my convictions, challenging the sincerity of my faith and the veracity of my writing, suggested I quit. Accusing words from the assailant pierced my internal fortitude, leaving me vulnerable and questioning my authenticity yet again. Cut to the core, my soul screamed for the midnight Visitor to reassure me again that He had bid me to bequeath my blessings. New growth was sprouting in Bible studies, published articles, and this book telling of my garden insights. It felt like the pruner was using a chainsaw on my sprouts.

It took long hours in the still darkness of a sleepless night to re-center my thoughts and to realize the adversity would strengthen me. It became a test of my "believing without seeing." I reminded myself that I was a new person in Christ Jesus, whether it was apparent to the angry pruner or not. It was comforting to me to know as a child of God that the One who lives in me is greater than the one who is of the world (see 1 John: 4:4). The pruner wasn't the evil archer as it appeared, but merely a bow used by my adversary to shoot unseen, but fiery, darts at me.

I experienced a night with my Lord that otherwise would have been missed while I slept. And when I searched my soul pantry for available comfort, I felt the joy of reaffirmation when I found it. Those stored-up promises of God were on hand when I needed them. The apostle Paul encouraged believers to use their faith as a shield against "the flaming arrows of the evil one" (Eph. 6:16). Never has his exhortation been clearer. Unprepared and unguarded, I allowed the verbal missiles to penetrate my heart. But the assurance of faith healed the wounds. Fresh buds emerged on my injured branch and my roots grew a little deeper. Pride took another critical blow as I tasted another sliver of freedom through the sorrow. An additional knot was released from the stronghold of my neediness. God can use all things for good, even careless pruners.

Leafy and Beefy

Fruit trees often grow so vigorously they become too leafy. The sun can't reach the interior branches. They may look healthy, but they don't produce enough fruit. It becomes necessary for the gardener to prune, cutting against the tree's natural tendency in order to produce more fruit. When left to themselves, grapevines and fruit trees generally favor new growth over more fruit. A wise gardener understands the nature of the tree or vine and knows when and where to prune.

My husband is the tree keeper on our farm. He periodically checks our trees, taking note of their growth patterns. In the beginning I questioned his methods (a dangerous thing in any marriage) when he cut off upward-growing branches. Removing a big branch when we so yearned for these trees to grow large, full, and shade bearing made no sense to me. Time proved him right. Removing a limb growing straight up redirected the energy to the outward-growing branches, and the tree quickly reached fuller proportions.

God works in every life uniquely. What He judges advantageous for me may be detrimental for you. My branches are different from yours, and we require different prunings. God stretches us individually according to His purpose. I may long to be taller and more visible and commanding, but He may want me to grow broader to provide shade, as was my husband's purpose for the trees at Cowlick Farm.

Even if we believe that God prunes us to get more fruit, our definition of fruit is often not the same as His. Making sure the sun reaches all the stems produces more flowers. Lush green foliage can actually keep the inner stems from getting sunshine and, therefore, stunt interior growth. Back when I learned this concept, I described in my journal a fully mature baptisia bush with a lovely deep green exterior that had bare stems underneath the bushy canopy. As I wrote, I sensed my Partner calling me to examine my own branches.

The luscious growth reminded me of my life's busy preoccupations that keep me from a more significant relationship with my Father. Pretty foliage, or worldly attributes, can cover up the bare stems—those places in our soul fields that need more attention. As a young adult, I surely tried to cover my achy heart by acquiring things and doing good works. I thought a canopy of goodness and rightness would shield me from unlove and would underwrite my worth.

Striving for intellectual understanding also retarded my internal growth at times, like the excess leaves, for God is not reasonable. His mercy and His ways are so foreign to mine that a logical worldview actually can separate us. Submitted to God, intellect is a gift for Christendom. However, my adversary can bend it into a weapon opposing the truth that God is holy love. Trying to intellectualize faith without grace is like washing dirty clothes in muddy water without detergent. Some of the dirt will dissolve, but the garments won't become clean.

I know a woman, Patsy. Good at many things, she feels no need to invite God into her private life, no need to be pruned. She regularly attends church to fulfill her spiritual obligations once a week. To her all is well because all looks well. Her body's beautiful foliage seems to defy gravity, and she looks more like a paid model than a mom. She drives a snazzy convertible, lives in the house everyone wants but can't afford, and even displays a rose garden with a paid rose-keeper.

Patsy doesn't see her neediness because she is too busy achieving success, seeking and receiving approval, and managing her assets. She also plays a killer game of tennis, has mastered bridge, and heads up the fundraiser for the art museum.

Additionally, Patsy walls herself off from anyone entering her soul garden. While friendly, generous, and outgoing, she rarely admits her needs. By admission, few have shared in her heartaches, though many are aware of situations that likely caused her suffering. Her excellence actually blocks her growth, just like the beautiful, lush grapevine with few, if any, grapes on the vine. She produces many worldly fruits, to be sure, but her inner stems stay barren. Her soul field lies dormant.

I am privileged to have been trusted to peek inside at her numerous unhealed wounds. I understand too well her attempt to earn self-respect and love. She strives for success to accommodate her need for self worth, and her achievements bring temporary relief. Just as putting a topical ointment on a migraine headache brings no reprieve, her worldly success cannot assuage the migraine in her heart. Her achievements mask her deepest desire to herself sometimes, and certainly to others.

She needs an expert pruning but is afraid to submit to her heavenly Father's shears. Even with all the admiration of onlookers, she remains destitute at her core. Having successfully charted her own worldly destiny, she is fearful and reluctant to relinquish the control of the remainder of her journey to God. It takes courage to let go of that which is familiar and has proven to be fruitful in our temporal lives. Because of my experiences, I can see clearly behind her walls, and with compassion offer encouragement. A piece of my regret is redeemed with every soul I comfort.

Timely Trimmings

By removing dead foliage, I improve my flowers' overall quality and future production. Pruning experts recommend cutting back dead stems until live wood is seen. The plant's energy then goes into producing more flowers, not more leaves. Some of us simply have too many leaves and not enough blooms.

As with the trees, without personal pruning, I won't reach my full potential. In the garden, I can snip off small shoots rather easily early on, preventing more extensive cuttings later. Similarly, if I clip away extraneous twigs in my life, my load lightens. I learned that perfect can be the enemy of good; striving for perfection can zap the joy of the moment. Also, by cutting back brittle regrets and painful memories, I save my soul from unnecessary struggles and jumpstart the rest of my journey. Pruning is actually God's answer to my prayer, "Lord, have Your way with me. I want to please You."

I often ask myself what defines me. Is it my business, appearance, friends, or neighborhood? Do the books, movies, or recreation I choose enhance my purpose in life? Do I identify myself merely by external activities? Who would I be without these definitions? These are questions to ponder as we consider personal pruning.

Scrap or Keeper?

It is through watery eyes that I write the lesson I learned about pruning. What has been painful to me, like the verbal attack on my faith, was not the result of God's rod, but His pruning shears. I had been looking for affirmation in the wrong place, from the wrong source. The untrained pruner attempted to cut the new growth sprouting from the book writing. But God used the episode to restructure me with His assurance.

It humbles me to know God finds me worth His discipline. He didn't necessarily cause the pain, but He surely allowed it to re-shape me. Over the years, He has cut off many shoots growing in the wrong direction or out of season, and now I thank Him.

The painful abandonment of a soulmate causing the breakup of our relationship forced new buds on a different branch—a blessing rather than the tragedy it seemed at the time. My dependence on her was redirected to the One who never disappoints or leaves me, and God's Word slipped back into its rightful place as my Authority and wisdom. Similarly, the forced retirement from my garden, a grievous disappointment, reshaped my purpose and priorities. Time requirements shifted, which proved to be beneficial.

An old friend unexpectedly called today and hearing the pain in my voice offered a timely word of encouragement: "God has found you worthy enough to prune." When gardening, I don't prune plants for which I don't have great hope. I prune the ones I expect to be very productive. Her reminder that God has plans for me lifted me up.

There's a story in one of my daily devotional books that evokes much prayer and contemplation each time I read it.

> An old village blacksmith once said, "There is only one thing I fear: being thrown onto the scrap heap. You see, in order to strengthen a piece of steel, I must first temper it. I heat it, hammer it, and then quickly plunge it into a bucket of cold water. Very soon I know whether it will accept the tempering process or simply fall to pieces. If, after one or two tests, I see it will not allow itself to be tempered, I throw it onto the scrap heap, only to later sell it to the junkman for a few cents per pound.
>
> "I realize the Lord tests me in the same way: through fire, water, and heavy blows of His hammer. If I am unwilling to withstand the test, or prove to be unfit for His tempering process, I am afraid He may throw me onto the scrap heap."[5]

Each year the message addresses a different test in my life and prompts self-examination of my fitness. My most difficult trials have shown me the sweetness and grace of almighty God.

Chapter 12

THE ENEMY:
SOUL TERRORIST AND
PEACE THIEF

Love your enemies.

—Matt. 5:44

WEBSTER'S DEFINES AN enemy as "… one hostile to an idea, cause, etc… anything injurious or harmful."[6] The Bible helps define our enemy. During His earthly ministry, Jesus described and warned us of our adversary many times. In my daily life, the enemy is anyone or anything that thwarts my spiritual progress or steals my bought-and-paid-for peace.

Many enemies keep me from achieving my garden goals. Hordes of insects can eat the leaves, stems, and very flowers themselves. They sometimes feast on my flesh! Polka dots along with middle-aged sunspots often riddle my body from the bites of the ubiquitous, marauding insects.

Every summer, Japanese beetles arrive in great strength to wage war on my zinnias that are just reaching their prime. These too-numerous-to-count raiders wear metallic copper and florescent-green coats. To battle these bandits, I strategically position traps and even engage in hand-to-hand combat. I either pick them off individually or scoop them into bags. They literally can destroy an entire full-grown zinnia within hours. In an attempt to thwart these robbers, I sometimes lose sight of the flowers and focus on, if not obsess over, this enemy (as I did with the weeds).

High Treason

One of my favorite things about living on a farm is the wildlife—my new neighbors. These citizens of the natural world fascinate me. I savor the unique privilege to observe their world up close. Through them, I have seen how even a beloved friend can knowingly or unknowingly play the part of an enemy.

In spring, one of my favorite neighbors becomes a garden enemy. Deer think my tulips and irises exist for their pleasure. And they use my sunflower sprouts for summer evening picnics. Years ago, in addition to the contracted tulips they devoured, I found four thrashed rows of irises soon after. The flowers appeared as if an army of two-foot-tall, machete-wielding warriors had attacked during the night. These deer munched the flower heads, leaving only inches of the stems intact. Telltale, pointed hoof prints left no doubt who the culprits were.

Additionally, my little furry neighborhood friend Peter, with all his cotton-tailed relatives, frequently feast in my vegetable patch. I enjoy watching the lovely creatures in the wild—away from my garden. However, when they damage my plants they become my adversary, robbing me of hard-earned produce and deterring my goal.

Pretty in Parsley

I well remember my initial encounter with the beautiful caterpillar. Wearing yellow and green stripes, it almost blended in with my parsley. When snipping herbs for dinner, I first saw the little striped warrior, so fabulously camouflaged. Had I not been wearing my specs and looking directly at it when it moved, I never would have spotted it. Unaware of its stinging bite, I removed it with bare hands, collected the parsley, and returned to my spaghetti sauce.

Back the next day, I found half the parsley bare—stripped of all foliage. Closer examination revealed several more caterpillars filling their little bellies. Wiser to the sting, with gloved hands I carefully picked them off and considered the job completed. But I was uninformed. The battle raged on, with a new battalion of caterpillars arriving each day. *Defeated—by caterpillars?* Frustrated, but determined, I got into battle formation daily thereafter. I aggressively fought this small, persistent adversary for the sake of the parsley.

Interestingly, these caterpillars, also called parsley worms, morph into black, elusive swallowtail butterflies. Some gardeners plant parsley for the sole purpose of attracting butterflies. To them, the caterpillars are not enemies but invited guests—another reminder that what is good for others may not be beneficial for me.

When my children were young, I had a kind neighbor with whom I enjoyed a special camaraderie. She frequently came by, shared her burdens, and wanted to chat. She regularly lingered in the late afternoon when I needed to shift my focus to my gathering family. Or she'd come by early in the morning when I was multitasking to prepare my kids for their school day.

I kindly explained that the times she visited weren't working. When she persisted to hang around during those times, she became like the caterpillar. Even though I enjoyed her company, the fact that she consistently intruded during guarded times made her presence detrimental to my goals. Tending my flock was my focus, and she compromised my efficiency. Her constant conversation robbed me of strategic time. I became grumpy when she kept me from tasks, and my family suffered the consequences.

The fact that I had to put on gloves to protect my skin from the caterpillar's sting creates another parable. How I deal with life's caterpillars requires careful and prayerful attention. The old adage "Handle with kid gloves" comes to mind. How to handle the dear neighbor required kid gloves and a heavenly Father's discernment. I needed God's character, compassion, and love—not mine. Removing the caterpillars must be tempered by keeping a vigilant eye on my eternal purpose, which is to please God.

Out of Bounds

In the garden, many treasured perennials (plants that return each year) spread so invasively that, like the cleome, I have to dig them up and move them to another space. The perennial, like my neighbor, is good, but when it reaches beyond its designated boundary, it becomes injurious to the other plants. It must be moved. That same kind neighbor who became an encroachment on my family's time may be a godsend to a lonely widower. However, the intrusion needed to be dealt with for my family's sake.

Though I love the beautiful rudbekia, or "brown-eyed Susan," even she had to be relegated as archenemy number one. While thousands of these versatile flowers bloomed in my garden, I discovered an infectious rash on my skin that resembled poison ivy whenever I touched them. I appreciated their value for my business, but my poor, itchy skin didn't share my feelings. A mere touch of a leaf caused an outrageous outbreak.

I decided to keep the flowers and protect my skin. At times I hired someone else to harvest them. Though definitely an enemy to me, they themselves were magnificent, innocent, and unthreatening. The flowers may not cause a rash in the next hundred thousand people they touch, but they were bad for me. The "rubies," as I affectionately call them, like the caterpillars, were just being what they were created to be.

Yet the rash robbed me of valuable time and comfort. It required much of my attention, demanding several visits to the dermatologist and the purchase of costly medication. It was a painful distraction. Many things in life are like the rubies. It can be my career, hobby, yard maintenance, computer, or physical fitness. I can even be consumed by church work or Bible study preparation. Like the rubies, these seemingly good activities can be infectious.

Certain relationships cause me to break out in a rash of unhealthy emotions too. When these rash-forming traits manifest themselves, I try to limit contact as I did with the flowers. Like my allergy to the rubies, it is a weakness in my system that creates the undesirable behavior. My desire for approval, not anything the other person does, may cause me to go along with a point of view I don't agree with or engage in an activity I don't enjoy. It can be a friend who pushes me beyond what I want or who encourages me to spend more money than I should. My critical nature emerges with certain people, while sarcasm or gossip sprouts with others. Each encounter causes me to feel a sickening disappointment afterward.

I am not saying it isn't good to venture outside my comfort zone and be with people who differ from me. Faith, by its very nature, calls us to live outside our comfort zones. For what is faith but trusting God when we are uncomfortable in the zone we are in? But wisdom calls us to identify that person, activity, or mindset drawing our attention from our intended course.

If attended for social appearance alone, to pad our résumés or create an image, even Bible studies and church may set off an outbreak. I have heard women speak of their church, priest, or Bible study as a private club used to command respect. Doing the right thing for the wrong reason can cause much confusion. Good activities create many costly detours on our journey through life. Fortunately, God uses even our self-imposed delays for our good, but hindsight usually reveals a better way.

The Nature of the Beast

The Bible says we have an adversary who prowls around looking for someone to devour (see 1 Peter 5:8). Jesus spoke of the Devil as a matter of fact, calling him a "murderer" and the "father of lies" (see John 8:44). He is also referred to as "the prince of this world" (see Eph. 2:2) and "the tempter" (see Matt. 4:3). To combat the Devil, Jesus quoted Scripture, as seen in Matthew 4:4, 7, and 10. He didn't retort with debates or ideas of His own, even though He was Jesus, the Son of almighty God. *Why do I?*

Smart, clever, and deceiving, our enemy often works by using a single thought. I have seen how just one negative thought, when left to run its course, can lead me down a destructive path. If I allow that thought to linger all day, by day's end I am annoyed, critical, or both. I lose the joy and peace that were mine in the morning. Similarly, one caterpillar on one leaf does not bode disaster, but allowed to stay it will invite the whole platoon. Eventually, if left unchecked, all the parsley will be stripped bare.

The enemy wants us too discouraged to continue. He works to frustrate our dreams and endeavors, always pushing God's people toward hopeless despair. He tries to dislodge us from our faith in God. He subtly interjects a doubt, which turns into fear of rejection, failure, or loneliness. The fear robs our joy. Without joy, we merely tolerate life, not celebrate it.

It is, therefore, imperative that we learn how to resist our adversary's attacks. Satan aims to divert us from Jesus. In my garden, the weeds, oppressive heat, and insects all provide examples of ways the enemy discourages me and draws away my attention. I repeatedly fought the temptation to abandon my desire to grow flowers.

Consider this example. At 9:00 A.M. a friend calls "Sue" to ask about the appropriate attire for the upcoming Derby party. Sue doesn't know because she wasn't invited. Right there the enemy spies an opening and craftily slips in through the crack, like a fly entering through a torn screen.

Why weren't we invited? We're almost like family, she thinks as she loads the washing machine. *I wonder if they are mad with us for not asking them to be godparents.* She continues her musing while loading the dryer. At 10:00 A.M. she wonders how many people were invited. At 11:00 A.M. she sees Suzanne talking enthusiastically to Jane at the end of the baked goods aisle and overhears, "It's gonna be fun!" At noon she passes her friend Debbie in the car, smiling while chatting on her phone. Sue's already encroached mind assumes Debbie is talking about that party.

At 2:30, rushing to pick up the carpool and feeling the onset of a headache, Sue sees Carol coming out of a shop with a hatbox in her hand. *She bought a hat for that party*, Sue decides as she ridicules her eight-year-old for singing happily in the car. At 4:00, Sue strategically calls Sylvia to invite her and Ralph for dinner on Saturday night, but Sylvia kindly declines due to prior plans.

"That does it! Everybody's going to that stupid Derby party but us!" she blurts while angrily (and dangerously) chopping onions for a casserole.

Later at 5:30, Kathie, her kind next-door neighbor (whom Sue assumes will most definitely be going to the party) calls. Exhausted from nursing her ailing mother while also coping with four small children, Kathie humbly asks a favor. Claiming a headache, Sue quickly declines, not wanting to expose herself to anyone who has been included.

By the time her husband comes home from work at 6:00, Sue feels rejected and insecure. Looking whipped, he announces he has had nothing to eat all day and looks forward to a nice dinner. She snaps at him while denying anything is wrong. He hands the mail to her, and what does she find? A smudged, crumpled up, obviously lost invitation to the Derby party. The humiliation her immaturity caused stings instantly. One faulty presumption robbed Sue of peace and joy all day, and negatively affected those around her.

Similarly, I too often take a negative word, action, or emotion from my husband and mull over it for hours. Each mulling constructs an invisible, but stalwart, wall between us. With each new negative thought I entertain, several bricks are added to the wall. I am quite adept at rationalizing the progression of derogatory assumptions and am confident of my brickwork! By day's end, I complete the wall, but he doesn't know why I am coolly uncommunicative.

My adversary relishes wall building, subtly encouraging me to continue, but my heavenly Father prefers tearing them down. I play right into the enemy's schemes when I choose bricks of pride, unforgiveness, and self-pity to construct a wall of separation.

Choosing kindness, gentleness, and patience instead builds a bridge that joins us. Jesus said, "I am the way," and His way takes me along the path of forgiveness, through the gate that connects me to the Father, who is Love. Gazing at the beauty of the flowers in my garden often became the simple act that refocused my thinking onto God's way. The presence of God in my midst often diffused my daily battles.

A Prowler

Our enemy is sneaky and devious. As Scripture says, he prowls about looking for whom he might devour. He does reconnaissance, searching for a weakness, to get a foot in the door. Always on the lurk, he waits for a negative thought, disappointment, or time of exhaustion. He stalks his prey like a lion waiting for an opportunity. He knows our flaws, needs, insecurities, and loves. We, on the other hand, struggle to believe such an enemy exists, much less guard against our stalker.

A negative assumption can also begin the parade of joy-robbing thoughts. For example, "Roy" may stress about how he can find time not only to mow the lawn, mend the broken fence, and get to the gym, but also to attend his children's soccer game and piano recital—all this weekend. This overload of activities may send him jogging mentally down a treacherous trail.

Negative thoughts squeeze him like an orange in a juicer. He becomes his own antagonist by telling himself it can't be done. Thereby, he plunges into a downward spiral that gains momentum with each item added to his to-do list. It indeed might be a physical impossibility to accomplish it all, but the battle is mental.

A change of attitude can save the day and, often, the marriage and family. Each of the items on Roy's plate can be a reason for thanksgiving—his children, job, home, and physical health. Or they can become stumbling blocks on his path. The choice is his. I saw myself in the same predicament in my garden almost daily. Completing the work seemed a physical impossibility, but the choice of attitude was always mine.

The first step is surely to recognize my vulnerabilities. What makes me feel insecure or stressed? In addition, where is my heart heavily invested? Jesus said in Matthew 6:21 that wherever your treasure is, there your heart will be. What do I treasure most? My enemy knows; I should too. I may chalk up my negative thoughts to being human, typically female, childish, or just normal. Doing that, however, allows my adversary the freedom to enter at will. Without the help of my heavenly Father, I may not look deep enough to see my weakness. Even if I admit to the possible vulnerability, I may be too fearful to risk exposure and seek help. I, therefore, provide fodder for the prowler.

In the earlier example, Sue was too embarrassed to confess her growing resentment. She thought that to admit it would further her humiliation in the eyes of others. Consequently, she got no help, even though her heavenly Father waited to heal her bruised soul. More likely, Sue probably thought her irrational emotions were a perfectly normal female thing, not of any spiritual concern. At that moment, her enemy won a small skirmish. He robbed her, though she wasn't even aware of the intrusion.

Similarly, when I stole the swimsuit as a teenager I rationalized my behavior by noting that other high schoolers did worse than I did. And I, like Sue, didn't want to risk further rejection by admitting my secret, rebellious thoughts.

I am especially vulnerable when it comes to family, my first, worldly love. Whenever my integrity as a young wife or mother was questioned, I overreacted. It took a long time for me to identify that since my heart was heavily invested there, my family was a likely target for the enemy.

I have fought many spiritual battles for my marriage and family because my adversary knows their importance to me. I don't care as much about success in other areas anymore, but don't assault my motherhood or wifedom! I determinedly have strived to be a godly wife and mother, and my spirit suffers a blow to its core when I am attacked in that arena. For that reason, I daily, if not hourly, submit my family to God.

My Medal of Honor—a Hug from God

A year after writing the first draft of this chapter, I have the privilege of safely harboring the memory of a toast my son made to me. On the eve of his marriage, at his rehearsal dinner last summer, he watered the garden of my soul. His generous words expressing his love and appreciation still feel like a baby-soft, chenille blanket tucked around my heart. I cried tears of thanksgiving, joy, and humility as he spoke, praising me for my sacrifices as a mom. I had suffered a terrible injury just a few months prior to the event. A severe case of food poisoning the very week of the wedding added to my weakness. I counted myself blessed to be alive, let alone present at this celebration dinner.

Only God's grace allowed this precious son to thank me, in full emotion in front of so many, for being his mom. All my mistakes and missed opportunities to strengthen, support, and guide him were forgiven. I was overwhelmed by God's goodness. I fought many skirmishes for this son's soul. Many times I witnessed his grief. But his words on that day made all the agonies of motherhood worthwhile. A quiet sweetness settled deep within the recesses of my spirit. My soul was at peace.

We had come to give the dinner for him, on his behalf, but instead I received the gift of love and appreciation. I was blessed in a very private, intimate way that defies description. Through this son, I truly believe my heavenly Father hugged me and gave His approval for my sometimes lacking, but sincere, efforts. He gave me a prize to take from the battleground of perseverance. It indeed was a sweet farewell as he left one family to begin another with his beautiful new wife.

My adversary failed at his attempts to rob me during that celebration time. From the pain, residual headaches, and confusion of the recent accident, to the debilitating poisoning, I was handicapped. The old energetic and enthusiastic me had slipped away.

Self-pity knocked again when I was left alone, and nearly left behind, at the hotel on the day of the wedding. Old Scratch still tried to snatch away the blessing I had received from my son the previous night. Dressing for the ceremony, I found I had not packed a particular garment that was critical to my overall mother-of-the-groom outfit. I readily improvised with a wanting substitute, finding security in the occasion for the apparel, not in its appearance. Had I not felt the assurance of a divine covering, I may have fallen apart with anxiety. I viewed the weekend as another sweet bouquet picked after frustrating days in the garden.

Sneak Attack

Imported accidentally to this country in the 1920s in the soil of potted plants, fire ants have become quite a nuisance. Quick to sting and ready to attack, the amazing creatures, though small, deliver a powerful punch. I have been stung too many times to count, my stings aching from swollen infections. These insidious beings took up residence in my garden and often brought my joy to an immediate, though temporary, halt.

My Teacher used even these six-legged intruders to enlighten me. They seem to multiply after a rain, their new mounds flourishing in the fresh, damp soil. In life, my adversary often strikes when I least expect it. When I have been rained on—bathed by the Holy Spirit—I become an easy target. My guard is down as it was after the toast that had lifted my spirits and watered my soul. First Corinthians 10:12 says, "Therefore let him who thinks he stands take heed that he does not fall." Perhaps I feel invincible after a time of peace and joy—fulfilled. But my enemies lurk, always ready to attack without warning.

We are called to suit up for spiritual combat daily. "Put on the full armor of God, so that you will be able to stand firm against the schemes of the devil" (Eph. 6:11). The attack can come from either end of the emotional spectrum—a moment of exhaustion can render me disarmed as well as a period of joyful satisfaction.

Many times after teaching God's Word I feel the Holy Spirit as surely as I feel the sun on my face. I bask in His pleasure and I glow with His love. My spirit at rest, I am at peace. If I received any praise, I can be sure that the prowler waits to pounce.

At these times, I am most susceptible to the enemy. When God answers my prayers, uses me, and lavishes me in His grace, soon to follow are self-doubts, questioning my motives, or feeling guilty for receiving praise. The enemy suggests, with a simple thought, that I am self-serving and, therefore, not worthy to teach. By allowing the thought to linger, I play into exactly what the enemy wants. By tempting me to disconnect from the Lord's graciousness, he attempts to stop me from teaching the Word, which I only can do by God's grace. Just one deceptive thought and my attention turns back on me, not God.

The Bible tells us Jesus was led away just after John baptized Him. When Jesus came up out of the water, He received His Father's praise: "This is My beloved Son, in whom I am well pleased." Immediately, the Spirit impelled Jesus to go into the wilderness where He fasted and was tempted by the Devil (see Mark 1:9-13). What a picture of suffering and temptation following blessings! Surely that proved true in my garden.

Armed and Ready

Through my garden enemies, God showed me that if I am careful, I will be stronger and wiser because of—not in spite of—the enemy. A self-appointed commander in the Special Forces, I have studied my garden adversaries' habits and created a battle plan. We know from history that great military generals study their enemies' characteristics. Since I've experienced my enemies' attacks before, instead of finding my zinnias nearly destroyed in late June I put up beetle traps in May. I am wiser and therefore armed. I anticipate the caterpillars and, ready with gloves and ammonia, halt them from destroying my parsley. We must do the same in our spiritual lives. Life battles are just as real as my battle with the beetles.

As a weightlifter employs increasingly heavier weights to build greater strength, God uses suffering as a catalyst for our faith. A soldier who has endured many battles is a better companion on the battlefield than a first timer, and combat is necessary for a victory.

Life is a combat zone, a constant battle between good and evil. In boot camp, officers simulate difficult situations to train soldiers. They especially teach them to obey their commanders unquestion- ingly. The sergeants create extraordinary trials in order to produce strong, effective soldiers. So it is with the training of God's army. I am learning to thank God for His boot camp and for equipping me to be a soldier in His militia. Being a Christian doesn't mean I will avoid heartache and trouble, but rather that God will accompany me through them.

We Are More Than Conquerors

Early one fall, I followed my heart and turned my barn into a marketplace. Wholeheartedly committed to this event, I prepared for two days of girly camaraderie, fellowship, and retailing (I hoped). Several friends were joining me and selling their wares as well.

Despite my best planning and hard work, the days prior had me feeling like I was in a tag-team wrestling match between Discouragement, Resentment, and Determination. I planted twenty large pots, cut and arranged flowers for selling, and scrubbed the barn, giving it a party face. I had less help than expected and little support. Much of the furniture I was selling required assembly, but the assistance I relied on never materialized. There was enough work to keep an enthusiastic team busy for a week. However, it turned into a one-man show. I was the one woe-man!

To accomplish what I had begun, my emotions had to be kept at bay. However, they often left the bay to rumble within me. The lack of help and support conjured discouragement and resentment. The two were worthy opponents of my resolve to succeed.

Dead tired at the end of the first happily successful day, I withdrew to the garden with a song in my heart. Thankful for a few moments of solitude before sundown, I slowly sauntered down a row of zinnias. As I moved, I stepped over what I thought was a stick. A few steps later, I felt strangely aware that I was not alone. There was no fear, but rather intuition.

I glanced back and saw that the stick was, in fact, a snake. Not poisonous, it nevertheless was neither invited nor welcomed in my garden. And it was large! I spoke to it as if I were speaking to another person. Looking back, I think I waggled my finger as Bernard so often had done to me. "What are you doing here? You are not welcome. You will not scare me away, nor will you keep me from growing these flowers. I am not afraid of you."

I normally am horrified of snakes, yet as the snake raised itself up and spread its "neck" out like a cobra in the strike position, I felt oddly empowered. Completely at peace, I ignored the show off, cut the flowers, and returned to the house with a bucketful of happy blooms.

We are told to resist the Devil and he will flee (see James 4:7). I resisted my fear, and it slithered away. Second Timothy 1:7 says we have not been given a spirit of fear, but of power and love and a sound mind. Again, I was reminded that He who was in me was greater than he who was in the world. If I have not been given a spirit of fear, then where does fear come from? Not from my heavenly Father, for "Every good thing given and every perfect gift is from above" (James 1:17). Fear is neither a good thing bestowed nor a perfect gift.

To me, the snake represented the internal wrestling match I fought the preceding week. I persevered, resolute to be undefeated, but I knew my enemy stood ready to steal my joy. He tried to wear me down and wanted to disrupt me, but my guard was up. My tag-team partner, Determination, and our manager, God Almighty, overcame the enemy. Paul encouraged the believers by saying we are more than conquerors (see Rom. 8:37). Walking in the garden alone that evening, I felt a sweet peace and confidence that all was well with my soul.

Be Not Fooled

The enemy uses fear to paralyze us in many unique ways. For one, the fear of failure pierces. Another may panic over rejection, loneliness, poverty, death, or loss of control. I must fight fear like a spreading fire, because whatever I dread controls me. My enemy uses my fears to grip me in his clutches. I know "perfect love casts out fear" (1 John 4:18).

No room for fear exists in the heart where Jesus lives, and it cannot coexist comfortably with love or faith. God's Word reveals who ultimately prevails over our enemy. I, by faith, must hold onto the power the Word holds for me. If my fear of snakes keeps me from my garden, then I lose. Moreover, if I stop growing and cutting flowers, the enemy wins. An ally of our enemy, that kind of fear isn't from God. The snake itself wasn't my real enemy, but a representation of an inner fear that could rob me of simple pleasures.

Knowing the truth defends against the Devil's lies, so I can be like the combat leaders who know their enemies. I must be informed and prepared in these perilous times. I am encouraged to "guard, through the Holy Spirit who dwells in us, the treasure which has been entrusted to [me]" (2 Tim. 1:14). Knowing the thief I'm up against, I safeguard my treasure, the abundant life. Jesus entrusted it to me. Since the Devil is the "prince of this world," I possess a natural tendency to judge my circumstances by the world. But I, as a believer, have a different standard.

The snake not only reminded me to be on guard always, but also that joy is mine as an over-comer. It was an intruder, but I still gathered a bouquet.

My Battlefield

We do not fight physical wars, but we fight spiritual battles daily. Ephesians 6:12 says we do not war against flesh and blood but "against rulers, against the powers, against the world forces of this darkness, against the spiritual forces of wickedness in the heavenly places." Ours is a spiritual battle to be fought with spiritual weapons. My battlefield resides in my mind and heart.

The conflict begins in my mind because my thoughts dictate my words, emotions, and, ultimately, actions. That is why we are told to "not be conformed to this world, but be transformed by the renewing of your mind" (Rom. 12:2).

When we study God's Word, it transforms our thinking. God's truth replaces old thought patterns. We begin to see things as God does and, subsequently, our actions change. God will not make me think like Jesus. Bringing "every thought captive to the obedience of Christ" (2 Cor. 10:5) is up to me.

As I practice submitting my thoughts to God, I also obey Jesus' command in John 15:4 where he says "abide in Me." Turning over my thoughts to a higher power fortifies me for all assaults on my life—physical, mental, and emotional. I need to keep the channel that connects us free of the condemning debris that plugs up my flow from the Source of truth.

The watering system for my garden rows occasionally developed leaks and plugs. When water passage was obstructed, the plants suffered from heat and drought. The water that could save them inadvertently was withheld. We also suffer when the enemy pinches off our source of spiritual nourishment. He craftily twists the truth like a kink in the water hose.

Once I began to grasp the rules of engagement, I had a new resolve. I looked at life from a different perspective. Walking through the woods, I keep a watchful eye for snakes and fire ants. In the spiritual realm I now keep a similar watch for deceptive traps. By far, the greatest attack on my home soil is in my mind. Few days go by that I don't put on the "full armor of God" in preparation for the day. I especially like the "helmet of salvation" (Eph. 6:17) as I ask God's protection over my mind. He is a faithful provider.

Chapter 13

STUDY AND PREPARATION: MAKING HIS ACQUAINTANCE

Be ready in season and out of season.

—2 Tim. 4:2

EVEN AFTER ALL these years since dreaded book reports were due and term paper deadlines loomed like threatening thunder clouds, I still squirm when told to study. However, as a novice flower grower preparing for success in my new career, I was forced to study. Learning about all aspects of gardening sharpened my understanding of the need to study Scripture.

Second Timothy 2:15 commands us, "Be diligent to present yourself approved to God as a workman who does not need to be ashamed, handling accurately the word of truth." Further along in 4:2, we are charged to "preach the word; be ready in season and out of season." How can I be ready to preach the Word if I don't know it? And how can it be available when I need it if it's not stored in my soul pantry? To have the Word of truth, I must read, study, and meditate on the message of Jesus, who is Truth. In the process, I get to know the Person Himself.

My garden tools provided a tangible picture of my readiness for God. If they lacked consistent sharpening, the blades' condition often reflected my spirit's condition: dull. Am I sharp enough to do the job? Do I need a tune up? Filing the blades will fine-tune my instruments. God will do no less for me if I want to be an instrument in His business. I need to be sharp—daily.

I have spent many an hour with my nose buried in a garden book, poring over the wise suggestions of those more experienced than me. Once I decided to become a gardener, it was the only sensible thing to do. I needed a firm grasp of the principles of gardening stored in my mind.

First, I read the words, trying to understand how they applied to my flowers specifically. Committing the concepts to memory, I carried the lessons into the field daily. Second, drawing from the knowledge, I attempted to practice what I read. Third, I observed the results and recorded my observations for future reference.

Through countless errors, I adapted the instructions to my specific climate and flower species. I wanted to be a wise gardener, not ashamed—I had spent too much time in my past with shame. Ready for the task, I strove to be informed. Intending to handle accurately the lessons learned, I humbly and diligently proceeded. A world of knowledge exists to anyone willing to learn, whether it be an earthly pursuit or divine comprehension.

Who doesn't prepare for whatever he or she is called on to perform? After all, we send our children to school for twelve years in preparation for life. Additionally, we often encourage four or more years to fine-tune their knowledge. We all learned reading, writing, and arithmetic in elementary school. But how much did we learn about our hearts along our educational path? What grade did we get in Advanced Compassion or Introductory Patience 102? In what class did we learn about marriage or parenting? Information abounds in daily conversations, novels, and mainstream media about the act that makes a person a parent. However, our society fails to glorify the heart condition and training needed for such an important role.

Similarly we provide our children instructions in soccer, tennis, piano, and horseback riding. Yet we are often slow to teach them to cultivate their spirit, plow their soul field, or gently soak their soil. We are made of more than just flesh, yet we tend to focus our time and efforts on feeding, educating, training, and entertaining the flesh. How malnourished we would be if we fed our bodies as infrequently as we feed our souls.

A Well-watered Garden

When getting to know someone, it helps to spend quality time in a variety of situations. Would you marry someone you didn't know well? I think not. Then why do we spend so little time getting to know our Lord and Savior, Jesus, with whom we plan to spend eternity? If we call on Him for help in times of need, shouldn't we know who He really is? Shouldn't we know what He thinks, requires, and offers us, as well as how we can please Him? Why is God worthy of my praise? What exactly has He promised in His Word? I've labored over these questions.

We read in Psalm 139 that "we are fearfully and wonderfully made" and that God knows us intimately. John 3:16 says God loved us so much He sacrificed His Son for us. If God loved us that much, then He surely wouldn't leave us without sufficient instructions. His provision, the Bible, resembles my flower-grower's manual, providing all we need to live abundant lives.

But storing volumes of horticultural books on my shelves fails to make me a better gardener. I must open the books, read the instructions, and practice the procedures. Even then, I still had to familiarize myself with the ins and outs of gardening before I truly was comfortable with it.

Our God has equipped us well for operation. Like a tilled and well planted garden, we have all the elements for success, but we need to be in close relationship with our Creator to know how our parts function.

Studying the Bible tells us about God, the Holy Spirit, and Jesus. However, until we open the eyes of our hearts, desiring a personal relationship with Him, we won't know Jesus intimately. To gain the intimacy for which we long, we need more than an occasional glance into God's Word. Teaching Sunday school and tithing our income won't foster closeness with Jesus. Keeping the Bible beside my bed or quoting Scripture won't do it either. The only way to fulfill my heart's need for God's cherished love is to spend time with the Master Himself. Meditating on His Word, relating to it, and practicing what I learn are necessary, but even the Bible itself can't save. It is the Person whom the Bible reveals that redeems me.

The Holy Spirit helps me understand the Word and apply it to my life. Like watering my garden, a gradual soaking benefits immeasurably more than dumping a bucket of water all at once. The plants need time to soak and gradually take up the moisture. Interestingly, when a torrential downpour comes, the layer of soil just under the surface remains dusty and dry. The same holds true of me. Voluminous study often leaves me overwhelmed, whereas spending time daily, if not hourly, listening with my heart soaks my spirit thoroughly. It requires quiet, uninterrupted time, even if only minutes.

My goals changed as my spirit awakened. I long for God's Word to touch my heart—not just my mind, ears, and eyes. In essence, knowing God intimately requires cultivation. It doesn't magically descend upon me like an evening fog. Peace of spirit won't grow overnight. It takes time, perseverance, and an honest commitment of my heart.

Help Wanted

When a team hears the coach's instructions in the locker room before going out on the field, a smart player puts into practice what he or she just learned. Our heavenly Coach gives us all the instructions we need, but He leaves the choice up to us. We decide the amount of time we spend studying His instructions, and we choose how to practice what we learn. A conscientious athlete will study films of his opponents, read playbooks, and mimic the greats, whereas another less-motivated teammate might neglect to research. The two could be equal in athletic ability, yet the one who studies to improve most likely will excel over the other.

In Matthew 14:16 and 26, Jesus promised that when He left, His Father would send the Holy Spirit to be our Comforter and Helper. God said He never would leave us nor forsake us. I want all God has offered me. I don't want to look back at my life, wondering why I tried to do it alone when God was there all along.

I easily can blame other people or circumstances for my problems (and frequently do). But in the end, I must look in the mirror of my soul and answer to God. He promised to walk with me. It was I, alone, who chose to go another way. His ways aren't my ways and I too frequently chose to question His instruction because it didn't satisfy my selfish desires. I surely have experienced many dark nights of the soul because I have walked away from the Light. It was not the Light that disappeared. It was I who chose darkness.

Similarly, in the garden I attempted the work without seeking advice from other gardeners. Until I desired more expertise, I was unaware of both the labor required and the help available. Simply knowing what equipment to have and how to use each piece made all the difference. The parallels, again, were striking. How much time and labor are we willing to expend for the harvest we desire?

Before I began reading God's Word using my new lens, I honestly thought my life centered around me. I now know it is all about God, getting to know Him and His plans for me. Comprehending His message is no longer one of thirty obligatory items on my to-do list, but a top priority, mandatory for survival. Because I am building a closer relationship to God, I purposefully set apart time to bask in His presence.

Chapter 14

SUPPORT:
SHARING THE LOAD

For the equipping of the saints for the work of service,
to the building up of the body of Christ.

—Eph. 4:12

FREQUENTLY IN THE dead of winter I cut branches not yet blooming, bring them inside, and put them in water. This encourages them to open up. The process is called "forcing." The branches I choose usually have small, tight buds, but no flowers. It is a glorious thing to have spring blossoms in my house in the dead of winter. All else is either covered in a blanket of white or looking like life is forever on vacation.

These buds in winter remind me of God's promises. Knowing what I'd become, He died for me while I was yet a sinner (see Rom. 5:8). I cut the budding branch, confident it will blossom. He sees me as a flower when I am only a bud. God gives hope when hope seems unrealistic. He gave sight to the blind (see Matt. 11:5) and promised us life though we were "dead in [our] sins" (Eph. 2:1).

My potential to bloom in my spiritual life may come in differing stages. Just as I watch the branches determining when to cut, God ever watches me. Psalm 139 says He knows me intimately. Only He knows when the time is right for forcing me. Some need little coaxing to bloom to their potential. Others require lots of time and attention. Still others simply refuse to ever open up and flourish. The opportunity is there for each of us, however.

Jesus said in John 5:24, "He who hears My word, and believes Him who sent me, has eternal life, and does not come into judgment, but has passed out of death into life." Moreover, we are told in Matthew 7:7 that to anyone who knocks, the door will be opened. He made provision for us, but we must choose to receive it. We can't just stand at the door. We must knock.

I especially like to force my quince, forsythia, crab apple, and pussy willow. It thrills my soul to bring these bare, ordinary branches inside my house in the cold of winter and watch nature do her thing. The stems show no sign of life other than the little notch, the beginning of a bud. All I have to do is provide the container and the water and eventually a blossom will appear.

God uses us as His container. We are but "earthen vessels" (2 Cor. 4:7) into which He pours the water. Since Jesus is no longer with us in the flesh, His Spirit resides in us (see 1 Cor. 6:19). We become His body suit. It is actually God, in me, who blooms.

Many Parts One Body

I have witnessed the way God uses us as His hands, feet, and tongue. When I was recovering from the riding accident, my friends worked together for one purpose: to support a fallen member. Each one offered unique support based on her own skills. God used each friend (the Holy Spirit covered with skin) to do His work.

What a blessing to see the face of my heavenly Father minister to me with such variety. For that season, I needed physical assistance and emotional support. It was inexpressibly heart warming to feel the love, encouragement, and back up of so many members. In another season, I hope to be the vessel God uses to pour out His blessing on someone else. Collectively, we are "one body in Christ" (Rom. 12:5).

We then, as faithful believers, become individual constituents of Christ's body, just as many individual plants make up one garden. God puts His spirit in our separate, customized "pots" and equips each of us for a different service. Our job is to obey the "still small voice" and go where He leads. "Since we have gifts that differ according to the grace given to us, each of us is to exercise them accordingly" (Rom. 12:6).

Two Realms, One Being

In the natural realm, our body is composed of three parts: flesh, soul (which includes the will and mind), and spirit. The flesh is the only part actually visible to the eye. My soul and spirit, however, are as much a part of me as my flesh, though you can't see them. When the least of my parts (perhaps a toe) hurts, I am altered. My whole body suffers to some degree. Similarly, when I have a nagging headache, I become less effective as a whole. I surely can adjust, but I am aware of the ailing member. Likewise, if my spirit, a vital but unseen part of me, suffers, my whole body feels the ache.

The spiritual realm is composed of the Trinity: the Father, Son, and Holy Spirit. Jesus, the Son, became Flesh, seen and tangible, and promised to send the Holy Spirit when He departed. That Spirit, intangible and unseen, needs a body to inhabit in order to act—to appear and reveal. We can't see God or the Holy Spirit, just as we can't see another's mind or emotions, but only the manifestations.

Created in God's image, who is three in One, it follows that we, too, are three in one. "Let Us make man in Our image, according to Our likeness" (Gen. 1:26). The word *Our* signifies plurality. Each member of the Trinity serves a different function, yet they are One, with one purpose. The Father sent the Son to provide the way to our heavenly home. The Holy Spirit comforts and helps on our journey.

I was reminded of this when I prepared flower arrangements. Only the flowers and the vase were seen, but the unseen water and oasis (providing sustenance and stability) on the inside were vital to the overall existence. Collectively, the individual flowers functioned as one arrangement. Each flower I used, however, had a particular assignment and was fundamental to the final image.

To grasp the message in God's Word, we must acquaint ourselves intimately with each member of the Trinity. Knowing *about* God will not get me to my destination. I need to know Jesus, whose footprints lead the way. And since His footprints are bloody and pass through much suffering, I can't follow Him without the Holy Spirit's help.

When any individual member of Christ's collective body is not healthy, present, or doing his job, the whole body weakens. First Corinthians 12:26 says, "If one member suffers, all the members suffer with it; if one member is honored, all the members rejoice with it." We, therefore, must acknowledge our membership in the body, discern our function, and perform our duty. God calls us to His body for a purpose, and He instructs us how to be good, effective members.

Are You Covered?

In my garden I planted three, four-by-sixty-foot rows of beautiful purple, pink, and white cosmos that grew tall, bushy, and multi-stemmed. They were in full bloom when a powerful storm struck, blowing them over on their sides. The stems strived to survive by turning perpendicular to the branch, which was then lying on the ground. They reached straight up, looking for the sun.

At the end of that damaging season, I investigated support netting. It had been recommended to me, but I had chosen to avoid the expense. I saw my error and checked my budget. The flowers I could have saved, and subsequently sold, would have offset the cost of the netting. I promptly placed an order.

The netting is applied over the top when the new plants are small, but sturdy, and growing upright. Posts on the sides of the rows support it. I used four-foot-long pieces of concrete-reinforcing rebar as my posts. By pushing the rebar firmly in the ground, I could stretch the netting and secure it tightly over the stakes. Each stem would be supported within one of the four-inch squares of the netting, as if surrounded by a four-sided railing.

It reminded me of a coverlet I had had over my four-poster bed when I was a young girl. I felt a sense of protection when I crawled under the canopy. Standing there in my garden, I pondered the analogy. God was again meeting me in my dirty overalls. I sensed His message, "I am covering you. You are My very own, and I will protect you. No wind will destroy you no matter how mighty. Allow the body of Christ to support you. Humble yourself and receive it."

At the time I was emotionally weary from personal conflicts raging in my life. I struggled to forgive perceived injustices and to heal bruised relationships. I questioned my own integrity to have allowed these breaches, and my joy faded. I felt unloved and unworthy again. Lonely.

Looking back at my circumstances, I was trusting my feelings rather than God. Dog-tired, I temporarily forgot I had been crucified with Christ and that it was no longer I who lived, but Christ in me.

Craftily using the situation to isolate me, my adversary subtly suggested, "You should do it alone. Nobody really cares and there is no one who can help you anyway." He always wants me unsupported and weary. I honestly thought no one could understand my circumstances, or would want to try. After all, mine was a beautiful life on the outside. Who would suspect internal strife? *With all the suffering in the world, I can't ask for help.* Fearful of being disappointed, I remained quiet. Stepping into the trap, I drudged alone.

Because the body of Christ is weakened when its members are ailing, we are called to "be kind to one another, tender-hearted, forgiving each other" (Eph. 4:32). James urges us to confess our sins to each other and pray for one another (James 5:16). Paul encourages us to build each other up (1 Thess. 5:11) and to offer support. I delighted to help others, but was hesitant to ask for and receive help myself.

In a remote corner of my soul, a trace of past perceptions remained; my confession and request for help would be a burden, not worth another's time. But I was ailing, and I longed for someone to bear the weight of my sorrow with me. Feeling trapped, I feared transparently sharing my grief would hurt those I loved. Again, I retreated and sought my Father who is the only One who can give me rest. He listened, and He used those ordinary metal support poles to remind me of His covering.

John Ortberg says in his book, *God Is Closer Than You Think*, "When you are unsure about a voice, go to some trusted friend and discuss it. Is this voice giving a true sense of conviction, or neurotic guilt? Lean into community."[7] Wounded and skeptical, I was hesitant to lean.

I have since seen how leaning can also strengthen the one leaned on. Like a weight added to increase my physical strength, helping others through their trials can increase my faith and improve my perspective of my own trials. It is often when supporting another that I hear God's words in a new way and am refortified.

The Higher the Ladder, the Greater the Fall

In solitude, I learned another garden lesson. The higher the plant, the more support it needed. A tall plant's stature meant it was more exposed to the elements and had more to lose. Likewise, the more things I accumulate in life, the greater the risk of loss. The higher someone climbs on the corporate ladder in the career world, the more he becomes a target. Increased money attracts people who want a piece of the wealth. A successful man is more likely to become the object of envy and jealousy than a simple pauper. Additionally, worldly success is a haven in which that old sneak, Pride, loiters.

The Bible teaches that to whom much is given, much is required (see Luke 12:48). Surely, God expects me to use the gifts He's given for the good of the body. However, I now see an additional meaning. Those who have been given much often need an extra portion of support. Those who stand tall are very exposed, because much is required *from* them.

Also, the great among us risk becoming proud, believing their success is their doing, not God's. Because it can be humbling to accept help, it's difficult for them to receive the support they desperately need. God requires humility for getting nearer to Him. He is "opposed to the proud, but gives grace to the humble" (James 4:6). The proud don't inherit the earth, the meek do (see Matt. 5:5 NIV). Thriving people often need help seeing this. I did.

We wrongly assume that someone who is successful by worldly standards does not need support. Surely the "nobody" in the world needs our prayers most. However, often the socially acceptable sin of pride causes the successful person to feel totally self-sufficient. He may think to ask for help would be a sign of weakness, which is likely his greatest fear.

When times of success grace my life, the enemy cunningly keeps me from seeing the potential danger. Thinking I can handle whatever comes along, I am discouraged from allowing someone to peek behind my façade. However, receiving help usually cripples Pride, which advances me several spaces forward.

Who's There?

Consider the minister who is worn out physically, emotionally spent, and feeling isolated. He thinks if he confesses his true feelings, others will not look to him for guidance. He fears his parishioners might think him not strong enough to be their pastor. Fear of losing his job looms. Those in his congregation may not offer him support, wrongly assuming he, of all people, can manage life's trials. He has all the answers for others and is in close touch with God—surely he can help himself.

Meet the president and CEO of a large corporation. He regularly makes difficult decisions that involve millions of dollars. He is the go-to man in the corporate world. Surely he doesn't need help, or if he does, he will hire someone. He spends more money in a year than I will make in a lifetime. He doesn't need my prayers. But this tall-standing man may be crumbling inside. He may be too prideful to ask for prayer, or too busy to see what's lacking. Blinded by his success in the temporal world, he can't imagine a need in the spiritual world. He may fall through the cracks, and not be included in our prayers.

I often have struggled to admit my wrongs to my children. I postponed my honest transparency out of pride as well as for their protection. However, even thinking I could continue to shield them was a subtle form of pride. *If they see my failure, will they no longer come to me as a trusted resource? Will they respect me less?* Yet it is paradoxically true that exposing our weaknesses strengthens others. Humility replaces pride, which is a great robber of healthy wholeness.

Those in high places need an extra measure of sustenance, even in our small inner circles in government, ministry, families, and local groups. Leaders of Bible studies, Sunday school, PTA, and at home all need extra support. Just like without support the high-blooming cosmos came crashing down with the storm, if we are not supported we too risk falling. Oswald Chambers says, "An unguarded strength is actually a double weakness because that is where the least likely temptation will be effective in sapping strength."[8]

The Support Trap

One early morning, the dew still clung to the ground and the air was refreshingly cool, but a distressing noise, like a cry for help, interrupted the tranquility. Arriving in the garden, I discovered a fawn trapped in the netting. He must have been rummaging for a snack and caught his hoof in the net. It took a lot of bending, twisting, lifting and coaxing to set him free, but I finally managed to do so.

Pete and Frances, my ever-present canine assistants, were very eager to help. Their enthusiasm complicated and postponed my freeing the fawn. After he ran off looking for his mama, I thoughtfully examined the ordeal.

What was meant for support for one creation became a stumbling block for another. We must be discerning in the timing and method of our support. That which enhances my worship time could possibly be a distraction to yours. How and where I worship is an individual choice. Praise, honor, and thanksgiving have many different forms of expression.

Additionally, the support netting made it more difficult to reach the flowers. I had to bend farther over the netting, which was uncomfortable. My back and thigh muscles notified me of their dissatisfaction afterward. It was also harder to retrieve a flower. Its leaves and branches tangled when I pulled it through the four-inch grid. Furthermore, if the poles didn't stay anchored or if they tilted to one side, the netting pulled them over as well.

Are we sometimes so supported (surrounded and crowded) that we cannot hear from God? Does the support insulate us from God rather than help? Is the care firmly grounded or is it leaning? I have interfered more than once in an effort to help only to later realize that I was keeping that friend from listening for God. I provided a "lean-to" instead of pointing to the "Rely-on."

Flexibility

Finally, we must be willing to allow room to grow. In the process of providing support for my flowers, I begin by placing the netting low on the stakes, just inches above the seedlings. As the plants grow taller, I slide the netting up the poles.

Similarly, the amount of personal support I give or receive varies with the season of my life. Sometimes I simply walk beside a friend, listening and sharing her pain. In another season, that same friend may need tough love or a call to accountability. Only by divine guidance can I discern how to adjust my support.

The promises in God's Word become our support and encouragement—our hope. Hebrews 11:1 says, "Faith is the assurance of things hoped for, the conviction of things not seen." We can't navigate simply by feeling and sight. Faith is required. Jesus tells us to be "shrewd as serpents and innocent as doves" (Matt. 10:16). A look at the word *shrewd* in *Webster's* gives us a rich perspective. Well down the list of meanings is "marked by cleverness, discernment, or sagacity: astute, keen (a ~ observer). Penetrating near the truth: knowing (~ guess). Sharp and searching (~ eye)."[9]

Ours is a world full of obstacles. We must have a keen eye to discern the difference between the truth and its perversion. Before Jesus advised His disciples to be shrewd, He warned that He was sending them out as "sheep in the midst of wolves." Jesus, the Good Shepherd, is alert to potential threats to His flock.

John 10 speaks of sheep knowing their shepherd's voice. When we know our Shepherd, we will understand we can trust Him with anything life throws at us. We must identify attacking wolves and listen for the still, small voice to guide us.

I am learning to recognize God's voice, but unfortunately, I don't always like what He tells me. I drift away in search of something more pleasing or an easier way. But, unsettled in my spirit, I ultimately return to His written Word. There I am reminded that God is my sufficiency (see 2 Cor. 12:9) and my covering (see Ps. 91:4). He is my hiding place (see Ps. 32:7) and my friend (see John 15:14). He is my protector, my confidence (see Prov. 3:26), and my support.

Chapter 15

HARVESTING: MAKING THE CUT

For I know the plans that I have for you.
—Jer. 29:11

WHILE READING MY journal notes, the spiritual parallels to the principles of harvesting all but jumped off the pages and marched around the barn. The timing of the cut, the method of the harvest, and the condition of the sheers combined with the gardener's knowledge and skill all affect the harvest's quality. Each consideration provided a unique look at my life from heaven's perspective.

Harvest time could be compared to the final line up in a beauty pageant. After matriculating through the long process of displaying their beauty and talents, contestants wait excitedly to be chosen. Several judges, with trained eyes, cast their votes, choosing the finalists. Drum roll…hushed anticipation…then…the announcement of the new reigning beauty. Exuberant applause erupts! The winner has been chosen, harvested, from the crop of contestants.

Harvesting refers to choosing and cutting mature flowers for my business. Careful to select the best specimens—flowers in their prime—I treat them with great care, ever mindful of the labor invested in them. How I value those special flowers chosen for my purposes.

Tried and True

As a new harvester, I studied the appropriate time to cut each type of flower. Sometimes the academic description of the stages didn't match what I observed in my garden. Something didn't fit, and I suspected it was my error, not the manuals'. This discrepancy left me questioning my methods. The process reminded me of a time when I struggled to relate to biblical personalities whose experiences seemed unrelated to mine. How could I realistically identify with Asenah, Bilhah, and Mahalath—whose names I could barely pronounce—or Abraham's Sarah who gave birth at age ninety? My wireless life didn't resemble their ancient existence.

In my quest to decipher the perfect harvest time, I searched garden books for professional photographs and asked other growers their thoughts on the optimum stage for harvest. I tried many different schemes, journaling my results. Eventually I learned to treat each flower individually, deciding when to cut each one independently. As was my habit, I spoke with my "children" as if they could hear me. After careful examination, I would say to one, "You need to wait till tomorrow. I don't think you're quite ready yet, but your brother here is perfect. I'll be back for you in the morning."

The times of confusion turned into seasons of reassurance. While putting the recommendations of others into practice, my faith grew. The flowers thrived as I entrusted my horticultural ignorance to the advice of experienced growers. It was a reminder to trust my Gardener's advice even when it doesn't seem to fit my particular circumstances.

The day I choose to harvest each flower may not seem obvious to a non-gardener because the blooms may not appear ready. However, after all my trials and errors, I know when the time is right. For example, a zinnia shouldn't be cut until the flower opens fully, but even then if the neck is not stiff the cut is premature. Sunflowers, however, are best cut before their flowers open, when the petals just begin to unfurl. The choice time for harvesting jonquils and irises is when only a pencil of color shows. If I wait until they are prettier, the flowers will have less storage time and vase life.

Ways and Means

Clippers also affect a cut flower's success. If the blades are dull, they will be more likely to tear the stem and discourage new growth. Just like a flesh wound to our mortal bodies, a smooth cut heals quicker than a tear. Dull flower cutters prolong my job, breeding frustration. God's clippers, which are sharpened to perfection, make accurate cuts, concise and efficient, and they never needlessly tear.

The method of harvesting can be as significant as the cut itself. Some flowers require cutting almost to the ground, while others need to be severed higher on the stem. Generally, the larger the cut (farther down the stem), the more plentiful the subsequent growth will be.

When cutting zinnias, for example, if I didn't need a large amount the following week, I cut the stems low to the ground. The premature shoots growing out from the main stem were sacrificed. If, however, I would need many flowers the following week, I cut a shorter version, leaving the remaining buds on the lower branches for harvesting the next week. I knew the plans I had for the zinnias. Cutting them low the first time looked severe but actually stimulated more growth. The zinnias don't know this.

A non-flower-growing friend watching me harvest my zinnias commented, "It looks like you are ruining them. Why are you wasting all those buds?" In life, our ways may appear ludicrous to others who don't know that we entrust our stems to our Master Gardener. Our wisdom, which looks like foolishness to them, is from God.

Chosen and Adopted

My stargazer lilies bloom only once a year. I keep a close watch so I don't miss my window of opportunity to harvest them. I must cut them no lower than six inches to the ground or they will not bloom the following year. It takes that much remaining stem to retrieve nutrients. Wouldn't it be great if we knew exactly what we needed to be productive the following year?

For most stems, a diagonal cut is preferable to horizontal. The slant creates a larger opening, which allows more water uptake. The literature suggests each flower's optimum location for making the cut. As with these flowers, I wonder if I am exposed enough to take up the blessings God offers me. Do I create a sufficient opening for Him? The cut would hurt if the flower could feel. Yet it is the cut that creates the opening to life-giving water. Similarly, cuts in life hurt, but pain draws us closer to our source of living water.

We all want to be useful and important, and we especially like to be chosen for our worthiness. However, we too often seek validation from the world. I spent much of my youth believing my actions would give me worth. But according to John 15:16, God chose me (just as I ordered my seeds) before I ever knew Him and proved my worthiness (which I couldn't do anyway). My adoption papers were already signed not because of my goodness, but because of Jesus' death on the cross. Back then I hadn't accepted them. Despite my new standing as a beloved child, I chose to live in a spiritual orphanage.

It is not for me, like the flower, to decide how or when I am used. Just as I choose which flowers to plant, grow, and cut, God, my Gardener, chooses how and when to use me. I cannot harvest myself. That is God's work.

When Am I Ready?

To be harvested in life means allowing God to reap what He has sown and grown in me. By submitting myself to Him, I allow

God to choose the time and place for putting my blooms—my abilities—to use.

Unexpectedly, my daughter was asked to be a small group leader for a larger Bible study she had been attending. She considered herself unworthy as well as too busy taking care of two small babies to do the job effectively. Yet she had been praying for God to show her what He wanted her to do. He called her, knowing better than she that she was ready for an early harvest. In another season, God may cause her to bloom elsewhere, for a different purpose. Like her, we can't know when the time is right, but Jesus does. We never will feel worthy because we aren't. Jesus in me is what makes me worthy.

I can't help but wonder how God sees me in terms of His harvest. Which of my "blooms" bring Him joy and satisfaction? What does He want to have sitting in a vase on His kitchen island? The whole Bible describes God's desire to bring His people to Him, like a homecoming or family reunion. He planned it, made our reservations, and arranged for our travel. The invitation is for eternity, but He makes kingdom life available to us here on earth.

However, God allows us the freedom to accept or reject His offer. Surely for Him, our worship, adoration, and obedience are a bountiful harvest. Even the desires of our hearts, if centered on Him, represent a pleasing harvest for God. If I am God's seedling, which He plants, weeds, prunes, grows, supports, and finally cuts, then He wants me to be beautiful—without blight or bruise. My job is to be the very best daisy, eggplant, or pumpkin I can be. God does the picking.

Choose Me, Use Me

If my flowers could talk, they probably would try to convince me to pick them. They'd urge me to recognize their beauty. *Surely*

I should be harvested today. But they wouldn't know of tomorrow's contracts, only what they wanted at that moment—the longed-for rest in the air conditioning away from bugs and weeds. Disappointed not to be the first chosen, they perhaps failed to realize I was saving them for a magnificent wedding reception centerpiece. Oh, how we try to preempt God with our nearsightedness and pride!

When I was a young mother, I rejoiced that God had harvested me for motherhood. I felt tapped. Chosen. Special. The day that concept gripped me was a joyful day. Though millions before me and millions after have been mothers, I sensed it was a calling and a gift. No longer did I search for meaning, purpose, or accomplishment with the desperation I had before. I felt a sweet sense of satisfaction. There is surely not much glory in being a stay-at-home mom, but I was in a special harvest season as God quietly used me. Being harvested doesn't always put me up front or in a position for praise.

Bring Him In

Since I see God's nature manifested in flowers and branches, I enjoy their presence inside my home. The God-made blooms redirect my focus from man-made trappings that fill my rooms. The flowers' monetary value on my table does not matter, but their effect can raise cold, rainy-day spirits to beachfront highs. Millions are spent annually in the ever-increasing commercial flower industry. Flowers are imported globally to meet the current demand. Perhaps everyone is unconsciously looking for God in the beautiful essence of the flower.

> O Lord, you have examined my heart
> And know everything about me.
> You know when I sit down or stand up.
> You know my thoughts even when I'm far away.
> You see me when I travel

And when I rest at home.
You know everything I do.
You know what I am going to say
Even before I say it, Lord.
You go before me and follow me.
You place your hand of blessing on my head.
Such knowledge is too wonderful for me,
Too great for me to understand!
I can never escape from your Spirit!
I can never get away from your presence!
If I go up to heaven, you are there;
If I go down to the grave, you are there.
If I ride the wings of the morning,
If I dwell by the farthest oceans,
Even there your hand will guide me,
And your strength will support me.
I could ask the darkness to hide me
And the light around me to become night—
But even in darkness I cannot hide from you.
To you the night shines as bright as day.
Darkness and light are the same to you.
You made all the delicate, inner parts of my body
And knit me together in my mother's womb.
Thank you for making me so wonderfully complex!
Your workmanship is marvelous—how well I know it.
You watched me as I was being formed in utter seclusion,
As I was woven together in the dark of the womb.
You saw me before I was born.
Every day of my life was recorded in your book.
Every moment was laid out before a single day had passed.

—Ps. 139:1-16 NLT

Chapter 16

POST-HARVEST CARE:
SPA FOR THE SOUL

He restores my soul.

—Ps. 23:3

AFTER NINE MONTHS of carrying a baby, labor and delivery may seem like the end. However, the baby's birth is merely the start of another leg of its journey, an expedition outside the security of the womb. The same holds true for cut flowers. Though guarded carefully while growing (like prenatal care for the unborn) and cut by a capable gardener (the obstetrician or midwife), a flower will fail to thrive if mistreated during the post-harvest time (childhood and adolescence). It saddens me to think of the many flowers I have lost due to careless handling.

Early in my role as a flower foster parent, I began studying the appropriate means of managing them after cutting. After all, it was my duty to prepare them for the world, as I had my real children. Water quality and acidity, as well as positioning of their containers, largely impact the flowers. Even the temperature of the room has great significance. Each of these considerations can influence their longevity and, consequently, their value. If harvesting was the final lineup in a local pageant, post-harvest activities could be the ultimate preparations to win the national title.

Time Out, Preparation, and Relaxation

The harvested flower has no plans of its own. Just like a newborn child, it has no agenda. Completely in charge of its care, I essentially afford my flowers a day at the spa in my not-so-salon-like, shabby she-barn. I want them at their best, rested and nourished, before sharing, selling, or presenting them for their final pageant.

The more I read both informational books and the notes in my journal, the more similarities I recognized between my cut flowers and me. Most flowers do best when given a rest period after cutting. I typically bring them inside and put them in a fresh water solution. Big five-gallon buckets keep them from being cramped or broken.

Next, I move them to a cool, open place. Before submerging them, I carefully rinse the stems and remove excess foliage to avoid possible vase-life decreasing contaminants. After a sufficient time of rest, usually a few hours to overnight, I re-cut their stems. This second cut stimulates additional water uptake, essential for longevity.

They, like us, need adequate fluid intake for survival. I have seen humans suffer heat strokes and receive intravenous fluid for immediate hydration. The flowers need similar treatment. After their fresh cut and re-hydration, I group them by color, size, or species and again submerge them in clean buckets for marketing. When making individual bouquets, I retrieve them one by one.

As I do for my flowers, I am learning to do for myself. Taking time to rinse in God's Word prepares me to be arranged by Him. I must remove the world's filthy contamination by allowing God's purification. For a while, I can wipe off the dirt. However, I, like the flower, can never make myself pure. The Holy Spirit in me identifies what needs to be stripped, like the underwater leaves.

Holy Hammock

God calls me to depend on Him for revitalization and replenishment, and to find my rest in Him. If I leave a freshly cut flower in the sun, even the strongest blossom will wilt. They all need fresh water and shade relief not to fade. Similarly, if I am not careful to rest under God's covering, no matter how strong I feel, I too will wilt. I often get so busy that I forge ahead without resting. I work, prepare, serve, and run all day. Distracted, I don't always take time to replenish.

Our Father calls us to rest in Him, and He warns us about getting overwhelmed. Jesus said, "Are you tired? Worn out? Burned out on religion? Come to me. Get away with me and you'll recover your life. I'll show you how to take a real rest. Walk with me and work with me—watch how I do it" (Matt. 11:28 MSG). Psalm 91 speaks of the "shelter," "shadow," and "refuge" of the Almighty where we are to "abide" and rest. And who wouldn't accept His offer to exchange yokes? "Take My yoke upon you and learn from Me, for I am gentle and humble in heart, and you will find rest for your souls. For My yoke is easy, and My load is light" (Matt. 11:29-30). What a great deal! Yet the trade off may mean setting aside my plans as I take on God's.

I spend a lot of time teetering between the "should-dos" and the "could-dos," but I don't stop to ponder what is important to God. Frequently, what seems pressing is not God's calling. Most of my busyness is self-imposed. When our culture encourages me to achieve and commit, I readily comply. But God calls me to be still and know Him.

God's holy rest is a state of mind and heart. His inner peace supernaturally permeates my spilling-over life. More than just an attitude, God's peace takes initiative. We can desire it, even pray for it, without ever achieving it. If I want a vacation, but never actually make the reservations and leave, then wishing for it does me no good.

The rest God calls us to take may mean stopping our busy-ness, even if we're not finished. Do our hearts really value peace? Jesus said He would go and prepare a place for us. I wonder if the soul at rest is a place He prepares while we are still in human form. To live the abundant life, there must be a place of abundance available to us. He promised to have a room in His Father's mansion waiting for us when we die, but He also has a room for us here. Now.

The author of Hebrews 4:1-3 says, "Therefore, let us fear if, while a promise remains of entering His rest, any one of you may seem to have come short of it." I frequently forget that resting in the Lord does not depend on what's going on around me. I have postponed it for days or even weeks at a time, in search of sufficient, available hours. Deceived by my adversary, I forget that resting in Jesus is always available. Twenty-four/seven. Weekends and holidays too. All I must do is go there.

Knowing my flowers need a rest period, I provide the place. I set them apart. It isn't an option for them, but a requirement of mine. As our Gardener, God commands us to come apart and rest. He set an example in the beginning of creation. Moses, the likely author of Genesis 2:2, says God rested from His creation work on the seventh day. The New Testament says Jesus frequently went away by Himself to pray. He took time to be alone with His Father. He found rest for His soul.

Preoccupied over either the past or future, we often miss God in the now. Worrying about what will happen tomorrow crowds my time. I fret over responsibilities, schedules, and demands. And I waste hours regretting my past poor choices. I too often live with an "if only I had" or a "someday, I will" mentality.

I have a friend who turns on her television when she is alone just to have noise in the house. She confesses her life is so hectic that the quiet makes her uncomfortable. Another friend told me that when her husband is out of town, she shops, travels, entertains, or visits, but does not stay home alone. Being alone with her thoughts makes her anxious.

Scripture mentions the word *rest* so many times that I believe it is not a suggestion, but rather a requirement. To grow in a closer relationship with our heavenly Father, we must rest. God calls us to relax, as in a heavenly hammock, allowing the Holy Spirit to blow over us like a summer breeze. Similar to molding to the shape of a swaying hammock, we are to conform to the sway of God.

The Caretaker

My flowers completely depend on me to strip their lower leaves and re-cut their stems. I provide fresh water, which has been amended for added strength and durability. My Caretaker provides the same for me but, unlike the flower, I have the choice to become too crowded, thirsty, or suffocated to receive His nourishment. Jesus said, "If anyone is thirsty, let Him come to Me and drink" (John 7:37).

I use a floral solution that improves the cut flowers' health. Soluble granules are manufactured with ingredients that can regenerate the flowers and prolong their vase life. When a quart of ordinary tap water is amended with a scoop of these life-enhancing elements, it becomes like the "living water" Jesus made available for us. It is what my soul craves.

He knows what I need for abundant life, and He offers me His living water perfectly amended for my growth. Jesus told the woman at the well that the water she drew would not satisfy, but the water He offered would bring eternal life. "Everyone who drinks of this water will thirst again; but whoever drinks of the water that I will give him shall never thirst; but the water that I will give him will become in him a well of water springing up to eternal life" (John 4:13-14).

Getting to know Jesus as a friend, my very own individual Lord and Savior—not my mother's, friend's, pastor's, or televangelist's

God—is only the *beginning* of the rest of my re-born life. It is similar to the harvesting stage of flowers. For them finally to be found worthy to be cut is only the beginning of their life. They were planted for a greater purpose.

Similarly, we were created to become God's children. The degree to which I accept His sacrifice on my behalf determines my success as a believer. It is a choice I make. Like a cut flower, I can remain in a bucket until I fade and die, or if I allow my Creator to market me, I can reach my maximum potential.

Some may consider their lives spiritually successful simply by believing in God. They may feel they have fulfilled their purpose. But if the flowers stay in the cooler at the barn, no one will ever benefit from their beauty. Our adversary wants us to hide our faith away, keeping our gifts to ourselves. He wants us, like the unused flowers, to stay in concealed buckets. While I gave post-harvest care to my beloved flowers, I had a different view of my purpose as God's child. I now see myself as a cut flower in His bucket.

Chapter 17

POST-HARVEST LIFE: SOUL FITNESS

Accurately handling the word of truth.
—2 Tim. 2:15

I N THE CUT-FLOWER industry, *post-harvest life* refers to the time after a flower has been cut, brought in from the field, and placed in a container. In flower trade manuals, the term refers to the amount of time the cut flowers actually maintain their loveliness. It is essentially the second part of their life above ground.

After their field life, they advance to a vase if they are successful. Many factors affect the well-being of a flower as it makes the transition. Sanitary containers critically influence the flower's health, as does the water's condition. Another aspect of the post-harvest dynamic is the atmosphere surrounding the freshly cut flower. As my flowers' caretaker, each of these considerations became important for me.

Because cleanliness vastly impacts the flowers' vase life, I carefully wash all my buckets with Clorox. The clippers need frequent disinfecting as well since they contact each flower. Just as a spoon can transmit germs, so can the garden clippers. Dirty utensils or containers can introduce bacteria, thus plugging the stems and killing the flowers.

As believers, we too should remove contaminated instruments and containers that cause bacterial build up in our souls. God never allows us to be tempted more than we can take. He offers us a way of escape, but the getaway is up to us (see 1 Cor. 10:13). I have choices to make regarding my soul health. I own my conversations and thoughts. Are they full of grace, replenishing me, or do my words and thoughts contaminate, weakening my faith? Self-pity and unforgiveness plug my stems and block the flow. The living water keeps me energized, but without it, I become weary before even beginning a task.

There are three basic ingredients in a healthy floral solution: sugar, an acidifier, and a biocide. Sugar feeds the stem. The acidifier facilitates the uptake of water, and the biocide kills bacteria. In the absence of a preservative, household ingredients can be substituted. I keep a liter of ginger ale, or any clear soft drink, on hand for my flowers. It acts as the sugar for nourishment. A drop or two of Clorox can be used as the biocide, and an aspirin for the acidifier.

I have often wished for a store-bought preservative for my soul. If only I could buy a liter of spiritual nourishment and sip it like a Coke! But then I would miss the process, which draws me close to God.

Another flower-longevity consideration is the location where they spend their post-harvest hours. Even the condition of the air surrounding the flowers is critical. Decaying fruits, vegetables, and nearby flowers can emit an ethylene gas, which damages the fresh stems. Fumes can be harmful too. Flowers do best when not in direct sunlight, or close to heat or air-conditioning units, which can cause dehydration.

The places we choose to hang out can do us great harm also. Being around a negative person can rob my joy if I am not careful. Vapors of sarcasm, gossip, or rudeness wilt me. My personal stems need a reliable resting place. The worries of life can dehydrate and cause my blooms to fade. Doubt muddies the water, weakens my faith, and slows my uptake.

Post-harvest life refers to the time after we make our decision for God, when we regularly relate to Him through Jesus. Making the initial commitment is only the beginning. God tells us He will never leave us nor forsake us (see Heb. 13:5). Paul said we are saved simply by believing in Jesus and receiving His Word as the truth (see Rom. 10:9).

However, our lives don't necessarily change visibly after that initial commitment. When I first decided to believe in Jesus as my Savior and as the way to heaven, I didn't feel different. Seeds were planted in my heart's soil, but they remained dormant for a long time before any visible growth sprouted. I didn't begin to experience my post-harvest life until the truth of God's Word saturated the soil. Seasons later, the truth demanded confession, and confession precedes forgiveness. Having acknowledged my needs and desires, I received God's forgiveness and was harvested as a cut flower.

When I learned the correct techniques of post-harvest life, I took great care to practice what I learned. I need to do the same in my personal post-harvest life. Jesus called it the "abundant life." I try to put God's promises into practice, "handling accurately the word of truth."

I can see clearly the need for my stems to be in a preservative at all times. I need the biocide that God promises me in His Word. He says He will be my "strength in time of trouble" (Ps. 37:39). I need the sugar for nourishment, which God's Word provides. His Word is life to me. I also need the acidifier to facilitate the uptake of blessings. My faith in God's promises is my security.

The Holy Spirit that dwells in me is my facilitator, my interpreter of the Word, ensuring my uptake.

The Mighty If

The word *if* is very powerful when God speaks to His people. Jesus made His promises contingent upon our actions. In His explanation of the Lord's Prayer, He said, "If you forgive others for their transgressions, your heavenly Father will also forgive you" (Matt. 6:14). God told Solomon that if His people would humble themselves, pray, and turn from their wicked ways, then He would forgive them and would heal their land (see 2 Chron. 7:14). Additionally, Jesus promised that if we believe, we will see the glory of God (see John 11:40). In each of these examples, God spoke to those living their post-harvest life, who believed in a saving God, and who had relationship with Him. The soul finds its home in God. When that place is found, the abundant life really begins.

When I made promises to my young children, I frequently made the fulfillment contingent on their behavior. "I promise to take you to the store if you get your homework done by five" or "I promise to make your favorite cookies if you help me clean up the yard" or "I promise to read you a book if you pick up your toys first." My purpose was to teach them about obedience, giving them choices. I used their chosen consequences to motivate their behavior. Similarly, the fulfillment of God's promises is subject to our obedience.

The success of our post-harvest life directly correlates to our contact with our Creator. If pleasing Him is our goal, then getting to know Him should be our aim. If we look to the world for our cues, we will not succeed in our post-harvest Christian life. Many counterfeit solutions, dirty containers, rusty clippers, and jaded purposes prevent us from seeing the lasting truth, and our lives will show it.

As a flower grower, I can predict my flowers' durability with reasonable accuracy. However, in my personal post-harvest life I have no such knowledge. I only know this life is a marathon, not a sprint. Hebrews 12:1-3 encourages us to "run with endurance the race that is set before us, fixing our eyes on Jesus ... so that [we] will not grow weary and lose heart."

I do all I can to provide for my flowers' fitness, both in the field and in the barn. I want to give them every opportunity to flourish. After all, that's why I planted them. Perhaps God sees us as His flowers for which He provides. He died that we might live, and He gives us post-harvest instructions. He rejoices to see us bloom and to be spiritually fit for His market.

Come as You Are

One of my favorite sources of buckets is the local supermarket. Since childhood, I have had an unhealthy affinity for the buttercream frosting used on birthday cakes. I began asking the pastry personnel for their empty buckets for my flowers, and they generously were willing to supply.

Occasionally I arrived before the buckets were washed, and I assured them it was acceptable to leave the remaining icing for me to rinse out. The number of cups of straight-from-the-container icing I have consumed in my car is shameful. I usually positioned the bucket on the seat beside me. While steering with my left hand, I kept my right hand working the bottom and sides of the bucket, scooping the sweet, silky-smooth remnants. As time wore on, I began taking my rubber spatula with me in the car for better efficiency!

The fact that the ordinary plastic buckets made the best containers for my flowers also compares to our post-harvest life. God comes to me as I am. He doesn't ask me to clean up first. He recreates me for His purposes, like how I transformed icing buckets into flower buckets. I am His bucket.

God tends to use the seemingly meaningless aspects of my life to flourish me. The ordinary becomes extraordinary when experienced with Him, which I witnessed when we moved to the country. In life's long process I never know what the next day holds, but I am confident of God's plan, and that is enough. "'For I know the plans that I have for you,' declares the Lord, 'plans for welfare and not for calamity to give you a future and a hope. Then you will call upon Me and come and pray to Me, and I will listen to you. You will seek Me and find Me when you search for Me with all your heart'" (Jer. 29:11-13).

Jesus said we "do not have" because we "do not ask" (see James 4:2). If we seek Him, He hears our prayer. He delights to bless us, His children. However, when we fail to approach our Father in utter surrender, we don't totally believe that He loves with a perfect love, so we "have not." We are looking through faulty lenses and hedging our beliefs.

Chapter 18

ARRANGING: POTTED PLANTS AND CENTERPIECES

Behold, like the clay in the potter's hand,
so are you in My hand.

—Jer. 18:6

ONE BEAUTIFUL JUNE morning, as I created a large arrangement for a special occasion, I listened to classical music on my little CD player. The symphony itself seemed to be in my barn. The notes floated eloquently in the air, magnificently enhancing my creativity and, therefore, my productivity. Swaying with the music as I worked, I dare say I felt like Mozart!

I strategically placed each flower in a vase in its floral oasis (a green water-retaining foam) saturated in water. For maneuverability I set the vase in the middle of my worktable in the center of the room. I needed to analyze the arrangement from all sides. I employed no particular rhyme or reason, but instead relied on my instincts.

Each selection affected the previous and subsequent choices, changing the arrangement. I didn't plan out what I needed ahead of time, but referred back to the overall creation. I couldn't have instructed someone what to do in my stead, or to say definitively why I chose a certain flower for a particular position. Yet I was confident as I progressed.

Occasionally a stem broke off, and I set the shorter version aside to be used differently. If the stem on the loveliest flower was not long enough to take the honored center position, I reserved it for the side. The small, almost unnoticeable flower falling to the bottom of the bucket was often the perfect choice for the front edge.

I sensed my omniscient Helper alongside me, just as I did when He appeared in the room with my newborn grandson. "This is how it is with you," He spoke to my heart. "You can't arrange yourself any more than these flowers can arrange themselves. As you do with your flowers, so I do with My children. I will use even the least of them to complete My masterpiece. If you break on your way to becoming the grand center, don't worry. I will use you in a different way, and for a greater purpose. I am the Master Arranger. I look at you from all sides and see angles you cannot see. I have had My eye on you since before you were born. Let go and let Me have My way with you."

Wow! How characteristic of God to perfectly illustrate His purpose in an ordinary event like arranging flowers. He speaks to us in a dialect we understand. At this time in my life, He reveals Himself through gardening. For others He may speak through parenting, merchandizing, laboring, or competing. He speaks through the stock market as well as through sickness. His means are as varied as our circumstances and His dialects are cross-cultural.

When the awe dissipated and my consciousness returned to the task, I continued putting the finishing touches on my masterpiece. However, my creation had a new, indescribable reverence to it, causing me to regard each individual flower with even more respect. After all, these flowers had made it all the way to the "national pageant," and each was eligible for the crown!

Then as I slowly ambled around the table, the overall creation appeared differently from each angle. Each separate flower had its own importance. No matter the size or market price, its function was necessary, and the overall display would have altered if even one was removed.

Many times, while arranging, the flowers fell to the floor and were damaged. I gathered them and created beautiful mini-bouquets from the unused pieces. A small vase of fresh flowers in my bathroom or on the windowsill above my kitchen sink brings me as much pleasure as a large, costly centerpiece. The little bouquet of leftovers reminds me of God's efficiency and how He uses me in the seemingly unnoticed and unexpected events of life.

Aren't we quick to strive to be front and center, attaching more value to that position? We long to be the main attraction in a grand ballroom rather than a potted plant on the floor. Important! Magnificent! I still sometimes measure my worth by whether I garnered recognition from my spouse, friend, or community. When I trust my Master Arranger to position me from His vantage point, rather than being short sighted, I end up with far greater value and beauty. It took many years of unrest for me to realize that titles and tiaras don't increase my value. My heavenly Father found me worthy before I ever made the first attempt.

Staying Connected

For the stems to survive they must be connected to water. To achieve this I must ensure that each stem is firmly inserted into the oasis, which acts as an anchor. I also must regularly fill the vase containing the oasis. Our heavenly Father offers living water and I, like the flowers, surely will die spiritually if I do not keep my spirit's oasis filled. Sometimes my personal stems are not firmly inserted, or not anchored, but seem to bob up and down. Spiritual dehydration sets in when I lose contact with my Oasis.

Over the course of time, a flower may lose contact with the water. The whole display can lose its appeal because one single flower fades or falls. However, the arrangement's overall life often can be restored simply by cutting and reinserting the stem or by removing it. The same is true in my life. If I lose contact with my heavenly Father, I fail, fade, or fall. The Bible warns that we may encounter stumbling blocks. "Woe to him … who would cause one of these little ones to stumble" (see Luke 17:1-2). I must replenish or remove anything that prevents me from soaking in His solution. Perhaps the hurt I'm feeling in life is merely God re-cutting my stem and re-inserting it into His oasis in a different position.

I am sometimes very slow to realize I have lost touch with my Oasis. Losing that connection causes me to dry up, weaken, or become an eyesore to the body of believers. In striving to be a good Christian, I am in danger of making Christianity my God, rather than worshiping the God of Christianity. However, since witnessing the absolute necessity of each flower's health for the good of the arrangement, I am quicker to identify myself as a fading flower, and reconnect with my water source.

Vases and Bodysuits

A vase is but a container for the flowers, just as we are only containers for the Holy Spirit. To be healthy, my flowers' containers must be clean—likewise, my spiritual well-being depends on a clean me. I, therefore, must choose carefully what occupies space inside my vessel.

The exact same flowers in one container can look completely different in another. I am learning to accept that my arrangement won't appear the same as my friends'. I have cousins whose beautiful, slender vessels can be threatening to an ordinary urn like me. I must fight to keep my covetousness at bay when we gather at the beach for reunions! All the more reason to fix my eyes on the Potter.

Some of my favorite flower containers are empty vegetable cans. Stripped of its paper label and adorned with a raffia bow, a can makes a very cheap and joyful floral package. A pineapple juice can last week, it now graces my kitchen island with irises and daisies. Sometimes God removes my manmade labels to prepare me for His ever more glorious use.

My accident badly bruised and scarred my container. Though I now sport a patched bodysuit, God's arrangement in me remains the same—if not more refined. Remembering that God looks on the heart, I am just as usable now as I was before. He's not daunted by scuffed vases and patched-up suits. Additionally, my leaky vessel is valuable in God's hands. His essence can ooze out of my cracks and brokenness.

Though God alone can make me genuinely lovely, I am not opposed to vase decoration. Sprucing up my body is fine as long as I remember the real value. Who resides within, what my attitude is, and where my worth comes from are what define me for God—not a fancy exterior.

I enjoy a makeover. The cosmetologist examines my face and skin type and offers hydration and color suggestions. I seek the service of a professional to cut my hair, and someone with a stylish eye to help me find good-fitting, well-fashioned clothes. They know which color is best on me, what cut suits my shape, and what style enhances my appearance. Similarly, I need to go to God for soul consultation. God is the expert and He alone knows how to beautify me inwardly. He is the ultimate cosmetologist, artist, musician, counselor, and stylist. I want to be a pleasing example of His handiwork, seeking His praise first.

Chapter 19

MARKETING: JUST AS I AM

Whatever you do, do your work heartily,
as for the Lord rather than for men.
—Col. 3:23

NOT ONLY DID I learn about planting, growing, and harvesting flowers when I started down this dirt road, I also learned about marketing. I always wanted to be chosen and used by God, but I never considered being "marketed" by Him. I now savor the thought that He is my agent. He knows how to maximize my potential, which He gave me in the first place. God has a position for me in the body of Christ.

Cutting the flowers begins their final sojourn with me. From the field, I escort them to my barn where I shower, feed, and water them. After refreshments, I reposition my tired blooms for a nap under an overhead fan. When rest period ends, I groom them, and then, last but definitely not least, I dress them for their new owners. Though they face an unknown future, they are now prepared for their new life.

Many a Saturday morning in a stand at a farmer's market I learned that more than just the flowers attracted customers. The location and design of my booth was also significant. And I was amazed that even my apron drew people. Numerous folks liked my handmade cow-print apron enough to inquire about purchasing one. And invariably people commented about my attire, which I thought was the worst part of my market presentation.

I assure you, my clothing was strictly for function, not for looks. I always wore my trusty, roomy, hide-a-multitude-of-stuff overalls and a sun-bleached tee shirt. As accessories, I wore an old faded hat and paint-spattered garden clogs exposing bare ankles still dirty from the early morning harvest. Quite often, I wore white cotton gloves (like the ones I used to wear to church and weddings) to cover swollen hands wrought with poison ivy or ruby outbreak. Folks gravitated to my booth and many favorably inquired about my get-up. "Where'd ya git dem pinklogs an 'at hat?" or "I wanna haf an aprin like 'at."

I also noticed the response to my flower bunches. I consistently sold more when I made bouquets, wrapped them in tissue, and tied them with bows. When I left the individual flowers in buckets, they were not sought. The flowers were the same, only differing in presentation. One customer said she favored the bouquets because they looked like a gift, and everyone likes a gift. Also, the bouquets already arranged could be put directly into a vase. Most customers preferred the bouquets made on the spot, customized to please the individual.

Each bouquet differed because I used no particular formula. If my flowers could reason, I would ask them to trust that I would use them carefully, artistically, and purposefully. Creating the marketed bouquets helped me appreciate my Creator and Marketer.

I shared these revelations with many of my customers as I designed arrangements for them. I explained how God uses us in His bouquets as I use the individual flowers in mine. He wants us to trust that He is arranging us according to His plans. They often left the booth feeling they had won the grand prize (and paid only ten dollars!). I later saw that God was actually speaking through me. My customers sensed His presence in His magnificently colored flowers, and that felt like a prize.

As I jotted these notes in my journal, I wondered about divine marketing in my life. Later, those particulars I noted at the farmer's market became lessons for life. When I let God do the arranging, what I give feels like a gift to others. In addition, if I freely offer without expecting something in return, it is ready for use. It doesn't need further manipulation. It is when I try to arrange and market myself that the product becomes less attractive.

Dancing Free

Discovering who I really am (as seen through a Heavenly lens) is the greatest personal gain I've received from getting to know God. It stirs up a joyous freedom that sparks loud singing and rejoicing from my heart. (I love living on a farm where no one can hear my opera-style, out-of-tune singing!) I tap dance on my front porch, and I regularly converse with my flowers, dogs, horse, deer, and other living beings. Free to be me, I shout to the Lord, and I love it! There is no one around to box me in or label, judge, or criticize me. Therefore, I am not tempted to conform.

Attitude Adjustment

My farm and garden companions, like my flowers, just are— they don't try to be. A great example of what God calls us to do, my dogs' unconditional love portrays God's nature. They forget my wrongs and hold no grudges. Always glad to see me, they don't take any of my grievances personally. They live each day as it is, without worrying about tomorrow. They don't waste time with self-pity. Like the flowers, they exist without attitudes.

Being myself frees me up for God to use more readily. When I am not afraid of what others will think, He can market me more effectively. Knowing God loves me unconditionally replaces my need to win the approval of others by being who I am not! Playing by the rules of this world exhausts—letting go of those encumbrances liberates. Releasing old, patterned programming may require baby steps at first. But like parents delighted to see their baby's first steps, our heavenly Father delights in our progress, no matter how small.

Proverbs 31 describes a virtuous woman as possessing great worth. She was well dressed ("her clothing is fine linen and purple," verse 22) and highly respected. Her life was productive as she cared for her household, both at home and in the marketplace. Her children "rise up and bless her; her husband also" (verse 28). She was rewarded with their praises.

But more importantly, this woman found contentment in her calling. Her attitude makes her appealing. Though committed to her work, she was free and confident in her choices; "and she smiles at the future" (verse 25). Not a fretter, she considered her field and reaped the benefits of her wisdom. Very marketable, this woman became my inspiration when I first read of her. As a young wife and mother, I aspired to be like her.

The woman in the proverb reflects an inner security by her outer expressions. Because of her strength of character (clothed with "strength and dignity," verse 25), her generosity ("she extends her hands to the poor," verse 20), and her prosperity ("her gain is good," verse 18), we sense she was very attractive. She appears the picture of one who is healthy, wealthy, and wise. Why wouldn't my heavenly Father want me to be attractive and successful? Earthly parents delight in seeing their children succeed. Perhaps our outward behavior and appearance is more important to God than we realize.

Marked and Tagged

Learning that my life centers on God, I realized that even my physical appearance reflects Him. If my objective at the farmer's market is to sell more flowers, then I need to be wise in how I market, package, and decorate my booth. If the cow-print apron appeals to my customers, they will be more likely to stop and chat with me—and perhaps buy my products. If sharing God's love is my worldly mission, my personal presentation is also of great importance. I want others to be attracted to Him in me.

I frequently receive catalogs from wholesale floral distributors. They often run special deals on plant tags, with encouragement to "be sure to tag your plants so your customers will know what they are buying." They often suggest using logos to personalize a business. Whenever I see the advertisement, I wonder what my personal tag would look like if I were a flower. What would my logo be? How is God tagging me for market?

I never would have guessed anything about my booth or gardening clothes would affect my flowers' success. However, when I left them untended in buckets at a neighboring booth one Saturday, not one flower sold.

Heavenly Buffet

We are all naturally predisposed to certain preferences. Some prefer blue-eyed blondes and others are smitten with brunettes. One person may love to chat the day away, while another prefers solitude. A northerner finds the heat of the Deep South oppressive, whereas the southerner basks in its comfort. And music that soothes my soul may send you running from the room. It is not that one is right and the other wrong. Rather, God created a wonderfully diverse mixture of human beings. He clearly is not boring!

God markets me by using my style, personality, and speech—all that are part of my particular make up—just as I use my flowers' colors, sizes, and shapes for an appealing display to sell them. He created an immeasurable assortment to fulfill His plan. Though my characteristics may not necessarily attract you, God has a place for them in His arrangement. If a financier is in the center, an artist may be needed on the side with an athlete on the edge. And when an entertainer is at the back, a deaf mute could be the choice for the front. It takes an infinite variety to complete His bouquet.

This smorgasbord of choices is part of the Master's plan. At the farmer's market, every booth had its own individual charm. The customers chose which booths to patronize. My job was to manage my booth and to keep it well stocked, not to force anyone to purchase my flowers. Similarly, in life I am learning to see myself as God's booth, custom designed and well stocked. Just as some flowers grow red and round while others bloom yellow and cylindrical, so do we. Seeing others and myself as God's handiwork, His special pattern, motivates me to be a fit expression of Him as well as curtailing my criticism of fellow travelers.

My CEO

God uses those portals—the five senses—to develop my individual presentation. They can improve my enjoyment of life by enabling me to hear from God and express Him in different ways. What I see, hear, smell, and touch are all means of experiencing His creation and being inspired by what I perceive. We are unique and colorful, each of us, and God wants to be the artist of our lives, using each individual palate He has provided.

Like a booth at the market, I am a mere storefront for God's blessings. Trusting Him as my shop manager and CEO—knowing He aims at something I cannot see—takes the pressure off. But if I don't maintain a heart for Jesus, at any moment on any day I can forget that it isn't all about me and stress reappears. Taking myself too seriously is bad for my mental and physical health. It also makes me less attractive, less marketable, and less enjoyable to be around. I don't even like to be around me when I'm thinking about myself too much! I, I, I, Me, Me, Me...It's wilting!

Investing Wisely

I am reminded of the parable of the talents. Jesus describes three men who are given a portion of a landowner's wealth to guard while he is on a journey. Upon the landowner's return, he rewards the two men who earned dividends, but rebukes the one who buried his portion for fear of losing it (see Matt. 25:14-30). God has given each person different portions, like different flower colors and characteristics. He desires for us to invest our share, our uniqueness, fearlessly, allowing Him to market us for the kingdom, not for the praise of others.

My portion may be creativity while yours may be musical talent and aptitude. Some are clearly more gifted athletically. Others, unable to swing a bat or kick a ball, can program a computer, conduct a symphony, or tailor a suit. In my estimation, humor is essential for survival, but many I love find it unnecessary. My daughters and I are drawn to what's stylish, whereas my sons and husband find the style-less perfectly acceptable! Whatever your portion, remember that God gave it to you for a purpose, to use it for His glory, and boldly trust Him in the process.

Stylin' and Smilin'

God sends us instructions on our marketing through the beauty of the natural world. He wouldn't robe His flowers in crimson and violet if He didn't want us to take a liking to the beauty. Artists forever have attempted to capture the magnificence found in nature. If the Creator lives within me, then I want to be "stylin" for Him!

A flower does not produce its fragrance and beauty on its own, but the flower's nature creates them. I want to display God's sweetness as the flower does by its fragrance, not by its might. I want to be so full of Him that it is no longer mine but His nature exhibited in me. No flower seeks praise for its beauty. It exudes loveliness by its very existence.

I had grand visions for the success of my flower business. But rather than accumulating vast earthly profits, I was able to share the simple truth of God's love in a tiny booth while scratching my itchy skin and wearing overalls. My customers became comfortable with me, the "flower lady," trusting my flowers to be healthy, long lasting, and worth the cost. We are to be marked by God's nature, seeking praise from none, but transparent for all to see God's love within us.

It takes a very close relationship with my Marketer to base my confidence totally on His ability. In my booth, I sold flowers. Another sold veggies, baked goods, and crafts. Mine didn't resemble others' booths, and their customers weren't necessarily mine. We all marketed our harvests, and it was not for me to judge any of them, their methods, or their hearts. Each booth has its own manager.

Chapter 20

PARENTING:
A DIVINE ASSIGNMENT

*Children are a gift of the Lord,
the fruit of the womb is a reward.*

—Ps. 127:3

I HAVE REPEATEDLY spoken of my flowers, seeds, and seedlings as my children. I value them individually, and I feel connected to each one. Because I plant, tend, and harvest them, I feel responsible for them in a parental kind of way. My female hormones kick in as I tend my seedlings, reminding me of my years as a young mother and reconfirming the principles I learned then.

God frequently uses my (human) children to teach me about myself. As a mom, I identified with God's parental role. I grasped the love required to discipline, and I felt the joy of watching a child grow in obedience. Yet when I disciplined, I frequently viewed myself in the child's role, with God as my Daddy. I recalled ways I disappointed Him with selfish disobedience and how He patiently waited for me, showing grace instead of exasperation. He still loves me unconditionally, though I don't deserve it.

Much of what I comprehend now through repetition in my garden I wish I had understood when my children were young, like pruning unnecessary activities that sapped my strength, or staying focused on my ultimate purpose, which was to raise wholesome children for kingdom life. Weeds of housework and ought-tos choked away my joy. No one would have suffered from an occasional unmade bed, dirty dishes left in the sink temporarily, or unfolded laundry remaining in the basket an extra day. Pride kept my focus on my agenda rather than on God's plan for their lives.

As my children tested their wings, my heart twisted to watch them fall. Yet I knew by nose-diving they would learn to fly, and eventually soar. Even as a parent, I fell headfirst. My heavenly Father watched me flutter lamely, though He had shown me how to ascend. I taught the lessons well, yet repeated the very mistakes I watched my children make out of greed, selfishness, or disappointment. Even as a grandmother, I still occasionally leave the safety of my heavenly Father's nest—nose-dive!

Heavenly Daddy

I asked my children to trust and obey me, thinking I knew what was best for them. Disappointment hovered— and even threatened my sense of control—when my advice went unheeded. God asks me to trust and obey Him as well and is surely saddened when I disobey. Jesus said that unless I become as a little child, I can't enter the kingdom of heaven (see Matt. 18:3). He is talking about a child's trust and confidence in his parents. My little ones trusted, believed, and depended on me because I was their parent. How much more should I trust my heavenly Daddy with all of myself?

Nothing is more humbling than to have my grandbabies bring their problems to me with total confidence that I will fix them. Without hesitation, they trust me to take care of them, like my flowers would if they were human. Whether it is catching them when they jump, tying a shoe, or providing a snack, they confidently trust my provision. A parental kiss can instantly heal a hurt, turning tears into a smile.

Jesus calls us into that same parent/child relationship. He asks us to trust Him without doubting, and to believe Him without seeing. He wants to be our go-to person. Until we see Him as such, we forever will try to fill our hearts' void. Just recently Henry, now three years old, brought his tangled knot of string to me. He struggled with it for a few, brief seconds before putting it in my lap and telling his younger brother that "Gee" would fix it.

Too sweet for words, his face was perfectly peaceful as he gave his problem to me. His simple trust pictures the heavenly statement "unless we become as little children." His assurance to his two-year-old brother, Ollie, innocently, but visibly, displayed his dependence on me. God waits for us to bring our tangled messes to Him and to trust Him to be the Untangler.

Unwrapping the Gift

Our children are a gift from God (see Ps. 127:3). They are not ours to own, possess, or recreate, but rather to love, nurture, instruct, and present to God. We receive our instructions from God and, with His wisdom, train our children in "the way [they] should go" (Prov. 22:6). Good parents, like good gardeners, are informed and diligent. They know which methods are necessary though are not always pleasing to their children.

As a gardener, I know what steps my flowers need to ensure a bountiful crop. My flower babies depend on me for their success. When, from the time they are tiny seedlings, I keep the end result in mind (tall, sturdy, cut flowers), I confidently do what is required. I must keep my focus, unwaveringly, on my endeavor. I imagine a young tree is never happy to see my husband approach with his pruning shears. However, it is proud of its majestic development when it reaches maturity as a handsome, shade-producing specimen.

How beautifully this parallels parenting our children. God admonished us to raise our children by His standards, depending on Him for guidance. I always knew I would be accountable to God for how I handled those precious gifts. When performing the daily, often thankless, task of child rearing, I tried (but often failed) to focus primarily on the end goal and not the hurdle of the moment.

God's last will and testament says He has prepared a place for us that is grander than anything we can imagine. It reminds me of the plans I have for my flowers and children, and their lack of knowledge of my purposes.

Rainy Days

As a parent, it's very difficult to allow our children to fail. I saw it clearly in the garden, where my flowers' success became a matter of pride. The better the flowers looked, the better I felt. I now painfully admit pride often motivated my striving for my children's success.

How tempting to help them cover up their mistakes. However, upon close examination of the Old Testament, I gleaned that God allowed His children to fail, falter, or stumble. They suffered the consequences of their actions or inactions. Many of God's chosen servants failed or suffered. Moses. Abraham. Joseph. David. Job. Each endured long and painful trials, but God used them mightily. Like these men, I am more likely to learn through adversity than if I simply sail through life.

One of my children, in about fifth grade, failed to prepare for a school project that had been assigned several weeks prior. After much reminding, discussion, and encouragement, the child continued to procrastinate until the eleventh hour. When he sought my help, I kindly refused and reminded that precious one that consequences would be reaped for his procrastination. I can't remember if he received a low grade, a failing grade, or a beloved teacher's harsh rebuke, but tears of humiliation fell from the little procrastinator's eyes. Being a student of high standing made it a painful embarrassment for him.

I well remember the comments of several friends who disagreed with my methods and the heartache of watching my loved one suffer. "How could you do that to your sweet child?" one said. And from another, "I could never let that happen. I love mine too much." Those words pierced my heart like poisonous thorns, and I quietly questioned myself and my wisdom. Later, I felt reassured when I remembered that life is a journey, a process, not a destination or a final goal. Our experiences are merely gateways through which we pass along the way. They are the chapters of our story. Gardening enlarged the entrance to my soul.

God calls us to provide an umbrella of love, security, and guidance for our children, which mirrors, in a small way, His umbrella of grace over us. At an early age, they should be given responsibilities and freedoms within the umbrella's confines. They need to learn that when they step outside that covering there will be consequences. It is their choice. Love's shelter always waits for them, but it won't move to accommodate their whims. It stays the same, like God's love and provision for us. Generations come and go, and cultures and customs change, but God's Word never changes. It's always available and applicable to our lives.

We can teach this most clearly by letting the rain fall on them early in life. Tough, yes, but better to learn over a fifth grade school project than later when the stakes are higher. A plant that spends its life in a greenhouse struggles to survive outside the warm, glassed-in haven. I see many parents sweeping in to protect their grown children from falling, trying to prevent the pain. They want to provide a perpetual greenhouse. Perhaps if the child had learned the painful, but realistic, agony of failure he would not need as much intervention. Allowing the child to experience the consequences of his choices is the job of the parent, not the child. Would a child ever choose embarrassment?

A baby eagle is pushed from its nest, high atop a cliff, to learn to fly. Although shoving the bird from its safe nest may seem harsh, it is an act of love by the mama eagle. In so doing, the baby learns to spread its wings and soar—likewise with the abandoned seed forced to search for nutrients on its own.

My tender young fifth grader is now a handsome, married, and successful man. Recently his company honored him for his outstanding performance in an ad in *Time* magazine. Though proud of his accomplishments, I saw the trusting face of my little child, a personal gift from God, in that magazine picture.

I still remember the sympathetic agony I felt watching him suffer the uncomfortable results of his actions. As an adult, he thanks me for the choices I made for him as a child—for the lessons he learned, and his sweet wife expresses her appreciation for the qualities she witnesses in him.

God uses this kind son, His servant, to assuage the inevitable bruises of regrets on a mother's heart. This grown child restores to me in loving gratitude what I may have lost in heartache through the trials of parenting. His words are for my soul what the amended water was for my flowers. I praise my heavenly Father daily for the inestimable richness he has brought into my life through my children. They are as the beautiful flowers I have cut after many months of tending and laboring over them in the garden.

The familiar old poem, Along the Road, portrays the value of adversity so well. In it, the poet describes how walking with "Pleasure" left the traveler "none the wiser," while a trek with "Sorrow" was invaluable. I committed each child to God when they were babies, knowing it would require they walk at least part of the way with Sorrow.

As a commercial grower, if I desire healthy, beautiful flowers I need to pinch off some buds and do a bit of pruning. In parenting, the philosophy is similar.

I missed many chances to instruct my children wisely due to my own self-righteous needs. Pruning, in the garden as well as in life, can drastically alter an image. Both my flowers and my children were off-shoots of me, reflecting my image. I feel overwhelmingly grateful to have the opportunity to redeem some of those mistakes with my grown children and with my grandchildren. By looking at my plans for them, I get an inkling of God's perspective. Regrettably, mine are flawed, whereas His are perfect.

No greater job exists than to so powerfully affect another's life. Parenting is an awesome, if not overwhelming, responsibility. It provides a chance to lead a little lamb to God, Who can save his or her soul. Though I relied heavily on God's wisdom and guidance, I wish I had trusted Him even more as I recall the past. My vertical lines of communication were obstructed easily by the events of life—my stems were clogged. I have asked for forgiveness from my precious children and my heavenly Father. They so graciously have forgiven me. The greatest thing I can give back to them is the wisdom I gained from my mistakes.

My Father provided my redemption through His Son's death and resurrection. I need only believe and accept. I cannot change the past, but I can give it to God and let Him use it for good in the future. I want my children to have everything of any value that is mine to give. If my disobedience and heartaches, my faults and darkness, bring enlightenment, then nothing was wasted.

Chapter 21

THE SHE-BARN:
FROM RAGS TO RICHES

Create in me a clean heart, O God,
and renew a steadfast spirit within me.

—Ps. 51:10

THERE WERE TWO tobacco barns on the farm when we bought it. I had an instant love for both of their dilapidated, nostalgic beauty. Traditional tobacco barns are typically sixteen feet wide by sixteen feet long by sixteen feet tall, window-less, and have a dirt floor and an approximately four-foot-tall door. Both of ours were typical.

At the first sighting, I knew I wanted to recreate one to be my garden home. When time came to tackle this project, my husband and I differed on how we wanted the barns to look. We also had dissimilar functions in mind for the buildings. I wanted one to be my flower shop as well as an eventual overflow bedroom when anticipated spouses and grandbabies began arriving. I wanted a haven for my garden and a retreat for myself. I had a clear vision. So in a brave, independent moment, I declared one the she-barn and one the he-barn, and I immediately began working on mine.

It soon had a stained cement floor (a firm foundation) and a loft, with a bed, sofa, chair, and desk. There is running water, and we added windows. An oversized entrance with an old-fashioned screen door replaced the initial opening. I whitewashed the interior walls, and painted the steps to the loft lime green and the upstairs floor a blue and white checkerboard. It is fully furnished from flea market finds and attic throwaways.

It is my sanctuary—a hideaway. I go to it in despair, joy, and exhaustion. I am revived there. Within its walls stirs a sweet, quiet presence. When summer storms strike suddenly and I hear the pitter patter of rain on the red tin roof, I feel its protective hug—like it has human arms.

As I see time's effect on my physical body, it delights me to note the pleasure this old, once decrepit, leaning barn still gives. I can testify to the restoring of my once worn-out and ready-to-be-abandoned spirit. Sitting in the shade produced by the fourteen-foot, wraparound veranda, I feel the Almighty's shelter. This old barn, used for drying tobacco in another era, is now being used to "cure" me!

Though you may find it cluttered and junky, to me it is comfortable and safe. There is an assortment of tools, baskets, pots, containers, stakes, hats, gloves, books, ointments, snacks, and one of just about anything else you could possibly want! It's an orphanage for my vast array of collectables, which don't have any particular value other than just making me happy. It is a place I can leave as is, and from where I walk away without having to clean or lock up. It is always there for me to go to sit quietly with my Father. No noisy machines or ringing phones interrupt my thoughts. No beeps, buzzers, or alarms. I have long conversations with no one visibly responding. My dogs and feathered friends accompany me and are always welcome.

This place is a picture of God—not in the physical, of course, but in its availability, provision, and simplicity. It was here waiting for me when we arrived, yet it looked essentially useless to the world's eye. I embraced it and now call it home. It mirrors my weary soul's transformation and reflects my conversion from dormancy to productivity.

I started out as the gardener and ended up as the flower, striving to grow and bloom. I began the barn renewal as the contractor and builder. I have ended up being built and contracted. Just as I had a love and plan for the old barns, I rejoice that God has a plan for me—also simple, leaning, and flawed—and is resuscitating me with His breath.

Chapter 22

HOLY HURTING: FINDERS KEEPERS, LOSERS WEEPERS

Consider it all joy.

—James 1:2

I'VE RIDDEN HORSES for about fifteen years, and the only thing adorning my head while riding has been a cowboy hat (or a flame-orange cap in hunting season). This past year my daughter, Katie, insisted I wear a helmet, and she gave me one for Christmas.

On a Monday morning in late January as I left the farm to teach a Bible study, I distinctly felt a disturbing presence, like hungry wolves surrounding me. The intuition was so chilling, I even visually surveyed the woods in search of intruders.

On entering the classroom at church, I whispered to my friend Katherine that I felt uneasy, as if enemies were encircling me. I was engaged in heavy spiritual warfare and needed her prayers. I asked to meet with her at the conclusion of class. As it happened, we both were detained in conversations afterward. With scheduled appointments to keep, we didn't pray together.

Returning home, I felt better, but still disturbed. In an effort to calm my inner rumblings, I headed out for a leisurely horseback ride. While striding toward the barn, an inner nudge warned me to return and get my new helmet. I obeyed the Nudge.

I rode a different horse than I was used to, named George. We were strangers, and I soon discovered his understanding of leisure was different from mine. Quickly, it ceased being a pleasure ride and became a power struggle. I soon knew I was in serious physical trouble.

George ran out of control, throwing his head, bucking, and trying to throw me. It felt like a monster was pursuing us, and George was running and kicking for his life. I almost felt sorry for him. Nothing I did changed his course. I simply had the misfortune of being on his back at the time. He abruptly slowed down, rose up on his hind legs as if to threaten an unseen opponent. I raised my arm up and called on God's angels to protect me. That is the last thing I can remember clearly before I woke up in the hospital.

When I awoke, I discovered I had sustained a severe leg injury. My neck also swelled with a nasty cut across my throat, making it difficult to swallow. The X-ray showed a pneumothorax (punctured lung). My horribly bruised body made every movement agonizing. A pounding headache and incapacitating dizziness were the result of a severe concussion.

By some accounts, I should have died. It surely looked like George had been the victor in that ordeal and I the loser. However, because of a God-given peace that "surpasses all comprehension" (Phil. 4:7), I didn't feel defeated.

Learning to Fly

My husband had come home from work uncharacteristically early that day. He saw George galloping by, sporting a rider-less saddle and dragging reins. By spotting George's return, he ascertained which direction to search and found me floundering in a field on the other side of the woods, about half-mile from our house.

I could have been anywhere, in any ditch, or under any tree on the more than two hundred acres of wooded space where I usually ride. Had he not come home when he did and seen George, it could have taken many hours, if not a day, to find me. He may not have even noticed my absence until dinnertime, when darkness would have made the search more difficult. I have a very vague recollection of hearing his far-off voice.

During the interim time of being thrown and being rescued, I experienced a rendezvous with our beloved dog, Pete, who had died two months prior. Somewhere in the midst of that inexplicable encounter, I also sensed my dad's presence. That visitation I remember with clarity. In the hospital and times afterward, the validity of the rendezvous story was questioned, due to the total amnesia I experienced regarding all the other details.

I distinctly remember questioning the reality of seeing Pete, even as it was happening. I knew he was dead, yet I was fully aware of his unexplainable but vivid presence in the bizarre moment. I remember laughing lightheartedly at the absurdity of it all. I even laughed at the fact that I was laughing, as if my condition shouldn't allow it. It didn't seem possible. Pete came up close, looked at me, and smiled as dogs do with his whole body and wagging tail. He remained there, very close in front of me, as if to prove it was indeed him. I stared with incredulity as he tried to lick me but never made contact.

I, of course, can't give proof of any of it. I only know it happened. We were bathed in very bright light during that happy reunion. I had a momentary sense of being too high above the ground, but without fear. It was delightful, completely carefree, and joyful. I wanted to touch Pete, but I couldn't move. My daddy's presence was not vivid, but merely sensed—a subtle awareness, like knowing someone is standing behind you in the check-out line without making direct eye contact. I do not remember coming back, leaving the light, or feeling any sadness. I frequently recall the total joy I felt, and it sustains me on my gray days.

I still wonder if I died for a moment before God gave me a new life with renewed vision. Did my immortal, unwounded spirit leave my injured, mortal body temporarily before returning to its retaining walls? Nothing at all about the accident itself stayed in my memory, but the encounter with those who had died remains vivid. My Savior uses this to teach me He is never far away, and that the heavenly realm can be enjoyed in the midst of earthly suffering.

Perhaps God, in His mercy, substituted amnesia for any memory that would have caused terror. In its place, He graciously allowed me the sweet experience of the lovely encounter with those dearly departed. My Father has guarded me from nightmarish recall.

Rather than preventing the accident, God protected me in it. He not only sustained me, He filled my cup to overflowing with His gift of renewed freedom. I became a participant in what, until then, I only had heard about: an out-of-body experience. Having tasted the other side, I developed an appetite for soaring beyond these restrictive temporal walls. Again, my Father gave me a jewel to take from the battlefield.

Singing the Blues

As I write this chapter, several months after the accident, I am still nursing this infected, painful, and slow-healing leg injury. My head throbs as I battle post-concussion confusion. I easily could have been permanently crippled, if not killed, yet I broke no bones nor suffered significant internal injuries. The pneumothorax spontaneously disappeared.

I don't know exactly what happened, but I know God allowed it, and He never left me. What lurking presence had I sensed in the morning before I left home? Was the accident an assault on my physical life by the unseen force felt earlier? Whatever it was, God used it for good.

What a miracle that I didn't sink into depression or fall prey to extreme anxiety! Before the accident, I was a healthy, active, independent, and energetic woman. I regularly tended my horse, garden, yard, dogs, husband, barn, and house. I played competitive tennis, and dabbled in more hobbies, plans, and projects than I ever could complete. I passionately babysat my grandbabies. I loved to cook, walk, garden, dance, bike, ride, work, and play, and often did them all in a single day!

I returned home after a week in the hospital unable to take more than a few painful steps at a time, even with a walker. I required a mechanical hospital bed, which was not receptive to comfortable, deep mattresses and pretty linens. I was unable to remember any of the accident, and I struggled with many thought processes in general. I was told I likely would start feeling "back to normal" in about a year. I required assistance for almost every routine task. In four months my two sons would get married in two different cities, three weeks apart. If I had not known that I belonged to my heavenly Father, I surely would've suffered a great defeat. By God's grace, I did not.

Every mom needs a daughter like my Katie. Putting her busy life on hold, she packed her two sons, both under the age of two, and came for ten days. She was able, like no one else, to speed my recovery. She fed, bathed, dressed, and loved me. She answered the phone, greeted my friends, and tucked me in at night. She never showed her frustration, only patience, gentleness, and kindness. She brought the babies to me for frequent cheer-me-ups, but never allowed them to be a nuisance. We laughed as she unsuccessfully attempted to beautify my bruised body. She blushed my cheeks, brushed my bed-head hair, and tied bows on my walker. She organized all the other earth angels so I'd have a caretaker each day and food in the fridge when she was gone. She appointed my friend, Janet, as arch-earth angel, with instructions to oversee all angelic activity. When she left, I wept.

Every fiber within me feels grateful to her, and I never will forget the beautiful way she gave herself so selflessly. I, again, felt my Father's embrace through one of my children, as His very presence embodied one of these babes I had submitted to Him. She had her Holy Father's eyes as she cared so willingly for me. And for her generous husband, my favorite son-in-law, who graciously allowed her the absence, I always will be so humbly grateful.

It has been a joy unspeakable to watch her become a godly wife and mother. Sharing the mysterious joys of motherhood with her blesses me beyond description. For this privilege, I never will be able to thank my Father enough.

A Late Date With God

Late one night after Katie had departed, I struggled to change the oozing bandage on my leg. That raw, angry wound screamed for relief. The horrific pain, dizziness, and pounding headache made my attempts extraordinarily difficult. I stumbled in the dark and fell. Very discouraged, I experienced more than a little self-pity.

Then I heard in my heart, "This is holy hurting. Don't ever forget that I saved you for a purpose. Whenever you see the scar, remember I am with you always." It was a spiritual encounter, not visual or audible, but genuine. My Midnight Visitor entered my reality again and His presence filled the room.

I tried to describe it to a few, but without much success. It was real, as real as the friends who brought meals each day, and I think I knew, even then, that the Lord was visiting me. My looming pity party turned into a holy celebration, and I actually rejoiced at the gripping pain. God took me out of my present emotionalism and drew me to Him. Renewed in spirit, I happily hobbled back to bed with the sturdy help of Ethel, my now bow-bedecked metal walker. Today as I write, my swollen leg aches and shouts to be healed, yet I can "consider it all joy" (James 1:2), for I know there is purpose in it.

From Victim to Victor

I am called to be an overcomer, for I am more than a conqueror (see Rom. 8:37) in Christ Jesus. This accident completely threw me off course, and re-routed and set me back for a season. Still handicapped and not close to pre-accident status, I am more determined to "be still and know" that God is with me. I do not fight my battles alone. Refortified, I hold tight to Him who is life, for I am one of the "partakers of Christ" (Heb. 3:14).

God used these difficulties to build my faith. He drew close to me in that time of suffering to mature my understanding of His ways.

After a while, I unexplainably welcomed my weakened state, believing God was strengthening me to be of service for Him. I saw the meaning of Romans 8:18, "For I consider that the sufferings of this present time are not worthy to be compared with the glory that is to be revealed to us." I, by God's mysterious power, knew without any doubts that He had been beside me the whole way, through it all. I have a sense of expectancy still—a joyous anticipation. The accident was not in vain, and I am re-determined to run in such a way as to get the prize (see Heb. 12:1). God re-plowed my soul and planted seeds for another harvest.

If I believe, then God is the Victor every time, in every incident in my life, whether it appears so or not. My restricted activity allowed me time to write this book, which I only had worked on sporadically previously. I now see that the time was ripe to fulfill my commitment to the Midnight Visitor. I believe God prepared me, like Esther, "for such a time as this" (Est. 4:14).

Looking from a different perspective, I reprioritized, renewing my desire to embrace life and not to sweat the unimportant.

Focusing on my eternal future diminishes the impact of today's glitches. The accident made me thankful to experience those uncelebrated pleasures we all take for granted. I well remember the exuberant joy of walking, unaided, to the front porch for the first time. I thrilled to feel the warm sunlight and fresh air on my face again.

Suffering is simply God's means of keeping us on a treasure hunt, always looking for Him. He has many jewels in store for us, and sadly, it's mostly in suffering that we see God's riches. Whatever thwarts me only provides an opportunity to see my personal Savior at work. God uses the Devil's very schemes to train me. Whatever cross I bear, if I bear it for Him, becomes a bridge connecting me to the One who died on it.

My Personal Trainer

Though I've logged very few hours in a gym, I have heard much about personal trainers. Hired to increase physical strength, fitness, and overall health, they aim for an improved version of one's physical form. The reference now has new meaning for me. I have a personal Trainer, a spiritual one, who puts heavy weights on me, assuring me of my growing strength. He asks me to weigh in daily to determine which exercises I need. Not at a certain time or designated gym, my workout sessions take place everywhere I go. I don't have to wear tight-fitting, bulge-revealing pants and tank tops. It doesn't cost a dime, but it does cost me myself. Then God mercifully gives me back a renewed self—and so much joy!

Chapter 23

CONCLUSION:
HIDDEN IN PLAIN VIEW

The heavens are telling of the glory of God; And their expanse is declaring the work of His hands.

—Ps. 19:1

THE STORY OF an old man speaking to God aptly describes us. In desperation he whispered, "God, speak to me" and thunder and lightening rolled across the sky, but the old man did not listen. The man looked around and said, "God, let me see You," and a star shone brightly, but the man did not see. He shouted, "God, show me a miracle," and a life was born, but the man did not notice. So the man cried out in despair, "Touch me, God, and let me know You are here." God reached down and touched the man, but the man brushed the butterfly away and walked on.

Nowhere in Scripture does it say God is fair, but many times it says He is just. A just God would not offer His kingdom to the rich and not the poor. Nor would He favor the strong over the weak or make His message so complicated that only the intelligent could comprehend it. It is accessible to anyone, like the air we breathe. Understanding His communication, whether through Holy Scripture or the visible world around us, requires eyes to see what is hidden in plain view, ears to hear God's whisper, and a heart ready to receive it.

I gazed at my garden flowers until their very beauty and fragrance became part of my soul. God wants me to absorb the exquisite colors and schemes of nature, for they are Him. I can't see God but I can feast on the manifestations of Him and the gift of Himself in all that surrounds me.

We humans can't fathom the almightiness, omnipotence, omniscience, omnipresence, and very essence of God's love. But having visited my Father so frequently in my garden, I see His creation everywhere I turn. His lessons show up in every task I perform on this farm as well as in the coincidences of my life, if I look.

As a young girl, one of my favorite hymns was:

Open my eyes that I may see,
Glimpses of truth thou has for me.
Place in my hand the wonderful key,
That shall unclasp and set me free.

Even then my soul's eyes searched for truths and life's mysteries. God drew me to Him many years ago, and perhaps He had this garden journey in mind all along.

Reading the Signs

I see His steadfastness in the daily sunrise and sunset. They are like perfect clockwork. The autumn leaves' brilliant colors and the flowers' velvet texture are a few examples of His artistic palate. The vibrant yellow, crimson red, and sky-blue birds' feathers display a hint of His creativity. The ocean, like a sea of dazzling diamonds when the sun dances on its surface, hints at His magnificence. His creation's shapes and sizes display His diverse imagination, as anteaters, hippos, raccoons, and penguins suggest His humor. The seasons and tides remind me of God's order. The mighty oaks' barren limbs in winter, which seemingly magically develop abundant green leaves in spring and summer, show His timing.

The dynamic strength displayed in hurricanes, earthquakes, and floods witness God's power. The wind we feel, but cannot see, reminds me of His omnipresence. The stars, which we only witness without the light of day, allude to God's perspective, offering glimpses of the treasures He provides for us in darkness. The garden's growth cycle portrays life on earth and all that is required for heaven. The fact that the sparrow thrives by eating only enough for today teaches me. The little acorn that grows into a giant oak, or tiny seeds that produce bountiful crops, bespeak His scale. Animals' protective camouflage, as well as each type's food supply, pictures God's provision and love. A friend to one is foe or food to another.

The way that a mother dog, lion, elephant, bear, or any other species knows to nurse, care for, and teach her young reminds me of God's sufficiency for all our needs. That a six-foot-tall human being came from a microscopic sperm and egg evidences a mighty Creator. The rainbow's magnificence far surpasses any manmade beauty.

God displayed His splendor graciously at our daughter Katie's wedding. She was married at Cowlick Farm on a knoll under the pines overlooking our pond. As the June sun gloriously stretched toward evening, I was seated to the hymn *Fairest Lord Jesus, Ruler of All Nature*. Since we sat in God's sanctuary, with hay bales for pews, I felt it a fitting song for the occasion. Surely, He is the ruler of all nature.

Another verse of the hymn describes Jesus as "robed in the blooming garb of spring." I used the flowers from my garden to decorate the sanctuary, and I felt we all were robed in His garb. It behooves me to know how anyone could doubt the existence of an almighty, creative God.

There was a sudden, almost mysterious, swoosh of breeze over the congregation when the priest blessed the bride and groom "in the name of the Father, Son, and Holy Spirit." A three-year-old child in the congregation of friends and family whispered to his mom that he saw Jesus.

Rise and Shine

As I lay awake in bed this morning, I listened to the birds chattering outside my window. What a fabulous way to wake up. Singing! Not stressing over the day's requirements, but singing. Robins also sing at night when their work is done. How often I go to bed feeling defeated rather than thanking God.

I love to watch my little feathered neighbors, for I hear my Father in their sweet twitters. Not a sparrow falls that our heavenly Father doesn't know about. These fragile little creatures take each day as it comes, without knowing what tomorrow will bring. They don't require a financial analyst, house cleaner, decorator, or physician. Perhaps their singing celebrates the simplicity of life.

A verse of the familiar old poem, "Overheard in an Orchard" by Elizabeth Cheney says it well:

> Said the robin to the sparrow:
> "I should really like to know,
> Why these anxious human beings
> Rush about and worry so."
>
> Said the sparrow to the robin:
> "Friend, I think that it must be,
> That they have no heavenly Father
> Such as cares for you and me."

Despite our technological advances, are we still not a people desperately searching for meaning? We are impressed by knowledge, yet we so easily miss our lives' real significance. Are the birds singing outside my window not more content than we?

I don't believe a single part of creation is a mistake. God can use even the most annoying or detrimental aspects of life to instruct and strengthen us. If we believe our Creator provides all we need, we will sing in the beginning and at the end of our days. We will grasp who He really is.

EPILOGUE

MY GARDEN BEGAN as a fallow field, but ended up as a sanctuary—a meeting place for my Lord and me. While attending service in this church without pulpit or pews, I heard eloquent, though strikingly simple, lessons. Much time has passed since I began this garden journey. Seasons in nature, and in my life, have come and gone, and I am both wiser and more humble because of them. I have slipped quietly from fifty-something to sixty-something.

Bernard is gone and is but a blessed memory in our hearts.

Lucy, a brown and white version of Pete, came into our family after Pete died. She happily accompanies Frances and me about the farm, though she cannot replace her unique predecessor.

My mare, like me, is older and more lame, but she remains a picture of tranquility as she grazes nearby.

George returned to the barn from whence he came after the accident.

Henry, the newborn whose existence birthed the call to write this book, is five years old now. I am still learning about God being the great Untangler through each of my five grandchildren.

I have not grown flowers for market since my accident. I do, however, continue to take long walks in the woods and am sure the same Someone hears me who heard me as a little girl. I discover ditch bank flowers regularly and am quietly reminded of the living God who is always near.

My shabby she-barn underwent yet another renovation, which is so fitting, for so have I. To celebrate the two new granddaughters added to my treasure chest this year, I painted the walls pink!

My two-acre garden has moved into a new season of life as well—it's now a driving range for my husband, complete with yellow flagpole and hole! In addition to becoming a better golfer, he is a pro of a granddaddy! Our course is changing as we approach life's back nine, adjusting our pace to a slower beat. Redemption's buds are emerging.

God keeps rewriting me as I painstakingly rewrite these pages, agonizing over the enormous amount of time invested. I am a different person now than when I began, and more scales have fallen from my eyes. My skin has more wrinkles, but I count them as joy too, for they came from a spiritual safari I would not have missed. I met Jesus in overalls, apart from my crowns and titles. There was no Cover Girl and no applause in the garden—just Him and me. In the beginning, I sought praise for myself to console my needy heart. But in praising God I found rest for my soul. He joins me when I live in a state of thanksgiving. I am learning to entrust every fear to my Father's heart, living under the umbrella of His grace.

In attempting to write, that I might give what was given to me, I journeyed back to the depths of my soul, retracing my past. It is one thing to remember the past, but another thing entirely to put it into writing. Exposing my heart was risky. But to love completely requires risking one's heart, becoming vulnerable. And to love well includes the possibility of being rejected.

I found that vulnerability, generally considered a weakness, became my strength. Entrusting my core exposure to God as I probed, ironically, validated me and, in taking the risk, I gained courage. I have recovered the heart that felt trampled, and I caught afresh the gentle rhythm of God's grace.

It was out of love that I asked what I could give my newborn grandson, and I believe that out of love, God nudged me to recall my story that He might lead me down a new passageway of redemption. I had no idea of that when I committed to write this book, that the personal journey I took while writing was part of the answer to my prayer.

Veering from my lonely path of searching, I found the unvarying lover of my soul. The world's grasp is loosening, freeing both my arms to embrace God—and life. His grace knows no boundaries. I can now move forward, on a different assignment, with a soul at rest because I know Who travels with me. My load is lighter and I am not afraid.

STUDY QUESTIONS

I'VE PROVIDED QUESTIONS for each chapter to stimulate individual or group searches. They are merely suggestions of things to consider; I hope you will find your own personal applications to the metaphors. Perhaps only one or two questions should be chosen for group discussion, as personal reflection can require much time and angst. Warning: Deep digging isn't for sissies!

Chapter 1: Hide and Seek (Read Matthew 7: 7-11.)

1. What is your heart searching for deep down at its core?
2. What personal secrets have you tucked away out of view? Why did you hide them from others?
3. What incorrect perception do you think people have of you?
4. What or whom do you fear most? What caused you the most anxiety in your past?
5. What one thing would you change if you could go back in time? Why? What difference would that change have made in your life?
6. Referring to the Parable of the Prodigal Son in Luke 15:11-32, with which son do you identify? Explain.

Chapter 2: Here Comes the Bride (Read Ephesians 5:1-2 and 28-33 and consider what God's design for marriage looks like.)

1. If married, what hidden bruises did you take into your marriage? Unknowingly? Consciously? If unmarried, what do you conceal from close friends or a potential mate?
2. What would you like to be pumped out of your past? Why?
3. How does your good behavior, morality, or work mask your need for God?
4. Describe your heavenly tab.
5. What does your amusement park look like? (What are the chief distractions? What "games" involve you the most? What rights do you hold on to?)

Chapter 3: Tick…Tock…Tick…Tock (Read Psalm 37:4.)

1. Describe a time you had to rearrange your heart and reorient your focus. How did you do it? (Alone, prayerfully, support group…?) How did it feel? Where was God in your life at the time?
2. Have you seen a God-given dream come to fruition? (What healthy childhood seeds are growing in your adult field?) Explain.

Chapter 4: Amazing Grace: Now I See (Read 2 Corinthians 12:9.)

1. Can you recall a time when you saw unmerited grace extended to you? Describe.
2. What faulty underlying assumptions have caused pain in a relationship (with people or with God)? What needs changing?
3. Have you seen your true identity through God's eyes? Give an accurate description.
4. Identify your needs. Are you in bondage to them?

5. How, or in what situation do you feel God's grace is not sufficient for you?

Chapter 5: A New Perspective (Read Jeremiah 31:17.)

1. Have you ever experienced a "divine appointment" with God? Describe and explain.
2. How does God show you yourself through the ordinary substance of life? Identify some "aha" moments.
3. Are you growing where you are planted? Describe the growth. Do you believe there is hope for your future as God spoke?

Chapter 6: Moving and Being Moved (Read Genesis 13. God blessed Abram because of his obedience.)

1. Have you ever been "moved" by God? What was the outcome?
2. In what condition is your "soul field"? (Consider: what do you do to cultivate it? How well does it drain after a storm? Do you enjoy going there? Do you avoid being there alone? Why?)
3. Where and how do you meet with your Father? How much of a priority is daily prayer and reading God's Word (on a scale of 1-10, with 10 being the most important)? Is it convenient? Pleasant? Uncomfortable? Why?
4. What is the biggest obstacle to your spiritual life? What keeps you from greater growth?

Chapter 7: Hoeing and Rowing (Read Hebrews 6:7 and consider yourself as "the ground".)

1. Was there a time in your life when you were plowed and broken? Who or what did the plowing? How did it feel? What grew as a result of the brokenness (flowers, weeds, despair, enlightenment)?
2. Are you an active gardener of your soul or are you a passive bystander?

3. What in your life is like the hardened upper layer of soil, hard to break through?
4. Rows need to be straight for future tending. What rows in your soul field are wavy (marriage, social, family, finances, faith, etc.)? How has it affected your row-tending?

Chapter 8: Seeds: Sowing and Growing (Read the Parable of the Sower, Luke 8:4-15.)

1. What is your personal soil type (rocky, shallow, thorny, rich, etc.)? How does God's Word grow in you (consistently, sporadically, seasonally, painfully, temperamentally, etc.)?
2. How securely embedded is God's Word in your heart? How was/is it planted in you?
3. Describe a time of darkness in your life. What did it feel like? What did you learn about yourself from the time of darkness?
4. Are you afraid to lose your identity and give up your comfort zone, if necessary, in order to grow?
5. What do your roots look like (shallow, deep, singular, branched, spread out)? What anchors you in a storm? What sustains you through rough times? Is it always reliable?
6. Do you feel adopted by God through Jesus? What did you gain from your adoption?

Chapter 9: Weeds: All That Grows Isn't Grand! (Read Ecclesiastes 3:1-15 as you think about the weeds in your life. I do intensive weeding in the garden on my knees. Go before God in prayer as you attempt to weed your soul.)

1. Describe how a weed robbed you of nutrients and water (joy, peace, rest, contentment, success, etc.).

2. What is out of place in your life, though not necessarily a bad thing, and needs transplanting? What makes it difficult to transplant? Into which row will you move it?

3. What weeds in your life have actually caused you to grow closer to God? Explain. Were you aware of their effect at the time or only later?

4. Identify a hardship you secretly wear as a crown or a badge. (We all have them.) How does it exalt or vindicate you to yourself and others?

Chapter 10: Composting: Give It Up (Read 2 Corinthians 5:17.)

1. What are your eggshells, peelings, scoopings, and coffee grounds? Are these sins or just encumbrances? What is the difference?

2. What keeps you from composting your scraps?

3. Do you struggle with brokenness? Why?

4. Do you really believe God will forgive you and cleanse you from all unrighteousness? Why? Why not?

Chapter 11: Pruning: Ouch, That Hurts (Read John 15:2.)

1. Describe a time in your life when you were pruned. Who was the pruner? How did you feel? How did you handle your emotions (hide, express, defend, deny, etc.)?

2. Pine trees are known to be self-pruning. Are you? (Do you require a constant gardener? Whom do you trust to prune you? Why?)

3. Are you too leafy? What are the leaves in your life? Have your exterior leaves stunted your inner growth? How? Do you have more leaves than blooms?

4. What is the purpose of your life? For what shape are you aiming? How will you know when you have attained your goal? Who is the judge?

5. How do you relate to the blacksmith's story? Do you fear God throwing you onto the scrap heap? Do you believe God uses all things for good for those who trust Him?

Chapter 12: The Enemy: Soul Terrorist and Peace Thief

(Read Matthew 5:44 and consider why Jesus said to love your enemies.)

1. What is your chief means of resisting your enemy (deny its existence, downplay its importance, recruit others to fight, confront, pray, distance yourself, etc)?
2. What keeps you from detecting its presence and understanding its detriment?
3. Give examples of how your mind distorted a simple thought. Name the things you lost.
4. How does the enemy look in your life? What outfits does he wear? How does he separate you from God?
5. How can we "love our enemies" while resisting them? How did Jesus do it? What can we learn from His examples? Did He die for them just as He died for you?

Chapter 13: Study and Preparation: Making His Acquaintance (Read 2 Timothy 4:1-5 and evaluate your readiness for God.)

1. How do you study God's Word? How are you preparing for the kingdom? Do you have a healthy workable knowledge of God's Word?
2. Are you prepared to "preach the Word" spontaneously?
3. What percentage of your time do you spend on spiritual nourishment? Compare it to the amount of time you spend on physical exercise, recreation, or personal relationships.

4. If you are a parent, how have/are you preparing your children spiritually? Is it a priority or an occasional lesson?

Chapter 14: Support: Sharing the Load (Read Ephesians 4:12.)

1. With what member of the body do you identify (head, arm, foot, toe, etc.) in your community, church, work, in the universal body of Christ? How has God equipped you for service in these areas? Attach a level of importance to each and explain why.
2. When have you experienced the suffering of the whole because of the hurting of a member (in your own home or family and/or in a corporate body)?
3. Are you better at giving or receiving support? Why?
4. Why do you offer support to others? What is your motivation? When have you provided a "lean to"? When have you encouraged another to rely on God?
5. Have you ever experienced a fall like that of the cosmos flowers because you were riding higher or taller than those around you? Explain.

Chapter 15: Harvesting: Making the Cut (Read Jeremiah 29:11-14.)

1. How has God harvested you? For what do you think He is preparing you? What stems are blooming or are at least showing buds?
2. How do you see yourself in the flower's role? What do you need in order to grow? What does the Gardener know that helps you grow? How can you capitalize on His knowing?

3. Does your self worth come from God? Explain. If not, where do you get it? Name the people, places, or things that give you a sense of worth. Are they consistently reliable?

Chapter 16: Post-harvest Care: Spa for the Soul (Read Psalm 23.)

1. How do you define rest for your soul? How does it feel? How often do you rest?
2. Are you still a flower in the bucket or are you being used in the marketplace? Who is using you? What is your purpose?
3. What causes you to wilt? To suffocate? What do you do to wash the dirt off your stems? Where does the dirt come from? Describe.
4. How often do you drink of the living water? Explain.
5. What do you want to do with the rest of your life as a cut flower?

Chapter 17: Post-harvest Life: Soul Fitness (Read Paul's letter to a younger Timothy, in 2 Timothy 2:15.)

1. How clean is your spiritual environment? Explain. What are possible contaminants for your blooms?
2. Name some "if" contingencies you have with others and compare them to God's promises. How do you respond when you read a promise from God? To what degree do you bank on it? How can you hold Him accountable?
3. In what ways has God taken something ordinary (like the icing buckets) and used it for an extraordinary purpose? Have you acknowledged it and praised Him?
4. What acts as the flower preservative in your life (the biocide, the acidifier, and the nourishment)?

Chapter 18: Arranging: Potted Plants and Centerpieces
(Read Jeremiah 18:6 and consider the words of the Lord telling Jeremiah he was as clay in the Potter's hand.)

1. Have you ever felt like an insignificant flower and found that God used you anyway? How did it feel? Did you see a divine purpose in it? Explain.
2. Do you believe God has a perfect place for you in His arrangement? Do you believe He is the Master Arranger? Explain why or why not.
3. How can you tell when your stems are out of water? Explain.
4. How well do you accept the container God gave you? Do you frequently wish you were like someone else? How do you think God feels about your container? Why?

Chapter 19: Marketing: Just as I Am (Read Colossians 3:23 and consider who you "work" for daily.)

1. What is your marketplace(s)?
2. If you were a flower, what would your tag say (hardy, perennial, seasonal, poisonous etc.)? How do you see yourself as God's expression of an attribute?
3. How does God show up in you? What does your "booth" look like?
4. In what ways/areas of your life do you see God as your CEO? In what areas do you push Him aside and take control yourself (business, marriage, parenting, competition. etc)?

Chapter 20: Parenting: A Divine Assignment (Read Psalm 127:3. Do you see children as a gift of God in today's environment?)

1. If you are a parent, what similarities do you see between parenting your children and your life as God's child? How

are you, in your role as the parent, like your heavenly Father? If you are not a parent, reflect on your relationship to your earthly parents and your relationship to your heavenly Father as His child in each of these questions.

2. Whom are you really protecting when you cover up for your child? How do you feel when your child fails?

3. How responsible do you feel for your children spiritually, emotionally, or intellectually? When can you let go? Do their actions reflect on you? What do you think when you see children of good parents do really bad things?

4. How do you think God feels when we do bad things?

Chapter 21: The She-barn: From Rags to Riches (Read Psalm 51:10.)

1. Have you ever had a she-barn renovation in your personal life when you took on a new purpose? What precipitated it? Describe the old and the new, the before and after. Does the "new barn" reaffirm you?

2. Consider: Is God calling you to leave something behind and to move forward with a new purpose? Is there an "old barn" in your life that He wants to refurbish (attitudes, relationships, patterns, habits etc.)?

Chapter 22: Holy Hurting: Finders Keepers, Losers Weepers (Read James 1:2 and consider the joy of the finder and the agony of the loser of faith.)

1. What scars (physical, mental, emotional) do you have that remind you of your purpose or goal in life? How do you view the pain?

2. Have you experienced spiritual warfare? Describe it.

3. What holy nudges have you obeyed? What was the result?

4. Who is your spiritual trainer? What is your routine?
5. Identify some weights God placed on you for your training. At what point did you recognize God as the Trainer?
6. Be sure to thank your Trainer!

Chapter 23: Conclusion (Read Psalm 19:1.)

1. Do you think God is fair? Why, or why not?
2. Where/how do you see His handiwork in your everyday life or surroundings? How do you read the signs?
3. As the robin asked of the sparrow, why do you think you rush about and worry so?

ENDNOTES

1. John Bunyan, *The Acceptable Sacrifice.* (Edinburgh EH12 6EL, UK: The Banner of Truth Trust, 2004), 115.

2. Oswald Chambers, *My Utmost for His Highest: An Updated Edition in Today's Language.* (Grand Rapids, Michigan: Discovery House, 1992), July 4 entry.

3. *Webster's Students Dictionary,* Copyright 1953 by G. & C. Merriam Co.

4. *Webster's New World Dictionary, College Edition.* Copyright 1962 and 1953, 1954, 1955, 1956, 1957, 1958, 1959, 1960 by The World Publishing Company.

5. L. B. Cowman, *Streams in the Desert.* (Grand Rapids, Michigan: Zondervan, 1997), March 4 entry.

6. *Webster's New World Dictionary and Thesaurus,* Second Edition. Copyright 2002 by Wiley Publishing, Inc., Cleveland, Ohio.

7. John Ortberg, *God Is Closer Than You Think.* (Grand Rapids, Michigan: Zondervan, 2005), 91.

8. Oswald Chambers, *My Utmost for His Highest: An Updated Edition in Today's Language.* (Grand Rapids, Michigan: Discovery House, 1992), April 19 entry.

9. *Webster's Third New International Dictionary of the English Language* Unabridged Copyright 1961 by G. & C. Merriam Co.

ABOUT THE AUTHOR

Jean and her husband live on their farm in eastern North Carolina where, though retired from commercial gardening, she continues to enjoy God through the natural world around her. Though she earned a BS in nursing from the University of North Carolina at Chapel Hill and practiced as an RN, her later years were devoted to a faux painting and concrete staining business. She is now a freelance decorator/consultant, encouraging others to renovate and enrich with a heart for God, seeing Him as the Decorator of our lives. Her family remains her preeminent occupation and dedication.

Whether splashing in the waves of the Atlantic, hiking mountain trails, or hearing the ubiquitous noises from the wild creatures in the woods surrounding her farm, she has a passion for God's living creation and the messages He continues to transmit through Nature. An active mother, grandmother, and homemaker, she cultivates her heart's soil through sharing God's love and insights with others.

She and her husband have three grown, married children and five grandchildren, with another soon to arrive. She looks forward to opportunities to speak and share from the personal harvest she reaped from her tilled soul field. Aware that everyone gets "plowed" at some point in their lives, she knows a healthy crop isn't always garnered from pain and brokenness. It is her desire that many would benefit from the lessons she witnessed as she allowed God to break up her clods and prepare her soul for planting.

You may contact her by e-mail at overallofus@hotmail.com.

9 781414 113852